THE $\mathcal{EX}$ FILES

To Write to the Author

If you wish to contact the author or would like more information about this book, please write to the author in care of Llewellyn Worldwide and we will forward your request. Both the author and publisher appreciate hearing from you and learning of your enjoyment of this book and how it has helped you. Llewellyn Worldwide cannot guarantee that every letter written to the author can be answered, but all will be forwarded. Please write to:

Rowan Davis
℅ Llewellyn Worldwide
2143 Wooddale Drive, Dept. 0-7387-1044-X
Woodbury, Minnesota 55125-2989, U.S.A.

Please enclose a self-addressed stamped envelope for reply, or $1.00 to cover costs. If outside U.S.A., enclose international postal reply coupon.

Many of Llewellyn's authors have websites with additional information and resources. For more information, please visit our website at http://www.llewellyn.com.

A *Zodiac* Guide to *His Former Flames*

THE *EX* FILES

ROWAN DAVIS

Llewellyn Publications
Woodbury, Minnesota

The Ex Files: A Zodiac Guide to His Former Flames © 2007 by Rowan Davis. All rights reserved. No part of this book may be used or reproduced in any manner whatsoever, including Internet usage, without written permission from Llewellyn Publications except in the case of brief quotations embodied in critical articles and reviews.

First Edition
First Printing, 2007

Book design and format by Donna Burch
Cover art © 2006 by Tracey Tucker/Langley Creative
Cover design by Ellen Dahl
Edited by Andrea Neff
Llewellyn is a registered trademark of Llewellyn Worldwide, Ltd.

Library of Congress Cataloging-in-Publication Data for *The Ex Files* is on file at the Library of Congress.

ISBN-13: 978-0-7387-1044-0
ISBN-10: 0-7387-1044-X

Llewellyn Worldwide does not participate in, endorse, or have any authority or responsibility concerning private business transactions between our authors and the public.
  All mail addressed to the author is forwarded but the publisher cannot, unless specifically instructed by the author, give out an address or phone number.
  Any Internet references contained in this work are current at publication time, but the publisher cannot guarantee that a specific location will continue to be maintained. Please refer to the publisher's website for links to authors' websites and other sources.

Llewellyn Publications
A Division of Llewellyn Worldwide, Ltd.
2143 Wooddale Drive, Dept. 0-7387-1044-X
Woodbury, Minnesota 55125-2989, U.S.A.
www.llewellyn.com

Printed in the United States of America

Forthcoming Books by Rowan Davis

The Ex-Boyfriend Book
(Llewellyn Publications, 2008)

I dedicate this work to all the women in my life who, due to various justifications and fears, I haven't yet taken the time to get to know properly. I'm sorry. And I'm trying.

Contents

Acknowledgments / viii
Introduction / ix

The *Aries* Ex-Girlfriend . . . 3

The *Taurus* Ex-Girlfriend . . . 19

The *Gemini* Ex-Girlfriend . . . 35

The *Cancer* Ex-Girlfriend . . . 51

The *Leo* Ex-Girlfriend . . . 67

The *Virgo* Ex-Girlfriend . . . 85

The *Libra* Ex-Girlfriend . . . 101

The *Scorpio* Ex-Girlfriend . . . 119

The *Sagittarius* Ex-Girlfriend . . . 135

The *Capricorn* Ex-Girlfriend . . . 151

The *Aquarius* Ex-Girlfriend . . . 167

The *Pisces* Ex-Girlfriend . . . 185

Acknowledgments

I could not have finished this work, or even thought to have begun it, if it hadn't been for all of the annoying, infuriating, and ultimately brilliant women who were the first to trample the generous heart of my wonderful husband long before I could get a crack at it.

Introduction

It's a universal truth that exes are annoying. However, using the principles of astrology, you can better understand what to expect when getting into a new situation with them. Some are more likely than others to cause problems, and some will do little besides make a minor attempt to regain the interest of their lost partners. Using astrology, you can understand the degree to which a person will go to ruin any new relationship her ex attempts to have, and even to hurt both the ex and his new partner individually.

There is one basic interest shared by most exes, despite their astrological sign: the desire for self-preservation, including one's self-esteem, ego, and social standing. A breakup can be hard on both parties, regardless of who actually left whom, and in reality few people remain friends with their ex-lovers. The negative feelings surrounding the division of a union—be it marriage, sexual, or romantic—are often projected on anyone who causes further friction, especially new romantic interests. This leaves people, who may have had nothing to do with the actual disintegration of the first relationship, dealing with a huge amount of the baggage. Because of the differences between men's and women's thought processes and their socially tuned responses to certain stimuli, many men are not socially savvy enough to help their new girlfriends deal with problems that arise from their old relationships. Astrology can help.

Elemental Tendencies in Relationships
Fire Signs (Aries, Leo, Sagittarius)

Fire signs are most likely to attempt to hurt both their ex and the ex's new partner individually. Fire signs are passionate people, whose anger and lust must fully run its course before dissipating. Sagittarius is the calmest of the fire signs and will rarely do anything in public against the new couple, but will use her own intelligence and independence to uproot an opponent while attempting to remain friends with her ex. Leo is the most egotistical of the fire signs, and will be loud and demanding in her newfound lack of influence in her ex-partner's life. Aries seeks to regain social standing and personal esteem after a breakup, and will promote herself and her new partner publicly while secretly plotting the demise of her ex's new relationship. Hurting her ex in particular is rarely a part of her schemes.

In general, fire signs are the most aggressive of the elements in the zodiac. Their presence as an ex can rarely be ignored, though one is always encouraged to try to ignore them anyway. Fire signs demand either submission or dominance from their exes and their exes' partners before they themselves are willing to go away.

Earth Signs (Taurus, Virgo, Capricorn)
Earth signs have a tendency to appear to be boring people at first. They are down-to-earth, sensual, traditional, and stuck in their ways. However, they are the most varied individual signs of any of the elemental divisions. Virgo is known for being open to many psychological disorders, Taurus is traditional and very earthy, while Capricorn has a tendency to dig for gold rather than for love. In general, earth signs are static people, and are easy to understand because of their simple desires and dislikes.

Capricorn is known for her adherence to socially accepted norms, placing her desire for money and status above any personal need for passion and love. She is most interested in her social position and will attempt to hurt her exes on that field. Taurus is very traditional, but somewhat able to accept new concepts. A lover of beauty and comfort, she is the most likely of the earth signs to make her partner comfortable and then outwardly ignore him after the union has dissolved. Virgo is loud in her hatred of almost everything. She is clingy and emotionally unstable, but will throw away the good with the bad at the end of an affair.

Air Signs (Gemini, Libra, Aquarius)

Air signs are the talkers and thinkers of the zodiac. They deal with philosophies, ideas, and the what-ifs of life. They lack the extremes of the other elements—the passion of the fire signs, the stability of the earth signs, and the emotionality of the water signs—but they combine certain aspects of each in small amounts within their own intellects. After a relationship has ended, air signs generally do little more than spread rumors, as they are rarely very attached to most of their partners.

Libra is perhaps the most emotionally driven of the air signs, as moods control much of what she does. She is in love with ideas and concepts, but rarely with actual people. She can admire, appreciate, and enjoy a person, but to love a man is too passionate and unstable and threatens to put her off balance. Aquarius is attached to people through her ego, not her heart, and is likely to seek revenge for any slights done to her years after the insult was given. She is the most aggressive of the air signs, and also tends to be the most disliked, as she does not have the social tact of Libra and Gemini. Gemini is more interested in the challenge of potential relationships than the attempt at cementing any current fling. In the rare case that she is honestly interested in keeping a partner, she can be manipulative, jealous, and hurtful if she is wronged. All air signs will attempt to get their exes back, if only for the sake of the challenge or preserving their egos.

Water Signs (Cancer, Scorpio, Pisces)

Water signs are emotional people who live in their own separate reality most of the time. When they are at their best, they can be wonderfully supportive and understanding. The Scorpio's reality is full of distrust, suspicion, and vengeance. The Cancer's is shaded and dreamy and comprises many people and situations that can hurt her at any given moment. The Pisces' reality is a watery world of self-serving people and situations, where the

Pisces is the victim in any situation and anyone that goes against her is bad and wrong.

All water signs lack a certain amount of accountability as well. Not one of them is willing to stand up and say, "Okay, I messed up here, and I'm truly sorry for what I've done," without intending that statement as a precursor to some accusation or manipulation directed at someone else. Any admittance of guilt is almost always followed up by a reason that they were not fully to blame, and how someone else shares the responsibility. When dealing with an ex, they are whiny, manipulative, and annoying people. They like to keep their exes around, just in case they need them sometime in the future.

An underlying factor in every water sign is the need for protection and stability, which can manifest as a need for control—gotten in any way possible that doesn't require too much work on their part. Cancer will rarely hurt her ex outright, or anyone associated with her ex, but instead will try to foster "friendships" that can be either emotionally draining or surprisingly soothing. Scorpio will try to hurt both her ex and her ex's new partner in any way she can. Vengeance is high on the Scorpio's list of priorities. Pisces will try to make her ex feel responsible for everything that went wrong in their old relationship and will use emotional ploys to manipulate her ex into harming his new relationship—either through cheating or through maintaining some lingering emotional attachment to her.

Quadruplicity Tendencies in Relationships

Cardinal Signs (Aries, Cancer, Libra, Capricorn)

Cardinal signs are the leaders of the zodiac. They have difficulty taking direction, criticism, or advice from others. They have a tendency to be more egotistical and socially adept than the other signs. As exes, they are most likely to target their ex than his new relationship or partner. They will try either to win him back or to retrieve their old social position. They can be underhanded in their attempts, but usually try to avoid any social stigma.

Fixed Signs (Taurus, Leo, Scorpio, Aquarius)

Aside from Taurus, fixed signs are the most devious and vengeful in the zodiac. They will try to hurt people rather than disband a new friendship or relationship. They all long for some amount of control, and are not subtle manipulators or plotters. Instead, they tend to be fairly open with their contempt, so their plots are easily uncovered.

Mutable Signs (Gemini, Virgo, Sagittarius, Pisces)

Mutable signs are unstable, and many take on the qualities of other signs. In general, mutable signs are changeable and easily influenced. They rarely stay in the same place for long. It's difficult to understand what group traits they have as ex-girlfriends, as all are more influenced by their element, gender, and the way they were raised. As a whole, one can say only that they are more concerned with control and power than with their ex or his new girlfriend.

The *Aries* Ex-Girlfriend

Dates: March 21–April 20
Planet: Mars
Element: Cardinal fire
Representation: Ram

A summary of the Aries woman can be made with two words: *rams* and *fires*. Just about anything that your mind comes up with upon hearing these two words is applicable to her. She's hard-headed, horny, craven, hot, and explosive...and also a ready scapegoat for herself. Imagine a flaming ram chasing you, and then brace yourself not to run away. Because you must *not* run away.

Hell has no fury...or so she'll want you to believe. And, she has a lot of the paraphernalia of the classical Hell to help her along: the stubborn ram and being the master of the fire signs. The only thing she has that isn't a part of classical Hell is Mars, which is the Roman god of war. Are you worried yet? She wants you to think that she's the biggest, baddest chick out there, and if you've harmed her in any way, watch out. What you *actually* think of her deliberate scare tactics is another matter entirely. If looked at correctly, an imaginary flaming mountain goat really isn't that scary—it's just somewhat destructive and kind of funny. The Aries' wrath is similar to the puffing of the big bad wolf—the stronger you are, the less it will actually affect you. If you're strong enough, you and your piglet (her word, not mine) friends might be able to eventually sit back and laugh at her from the safety of your brick personality. If you're weak, however, your new vocation in life will be as a supplier of cow fodder.

As a romantic partner, the Aries woman was explosively defensive of her man. If he encountered any criticism at work or from friends, she'd immediately jump to his side, wielding a flaming sword and decked in the shiniest of white armor—even if she privately thought that the negativity aimed at him was well deserved. She has difficulty being with a man who is not respected by his peers, and she tried to change any quality in him that could summon derision in others.

Aries women search for either established men who can provide opportunities for them (but not provide *everything* for them, because no Aries will allow a man to impinge on her freedom) or clay-men whom they can mold and fire in their red-hot kiln. You're lucky, in a way, if you have the second type. Men who are well established and who dated a randy Aries got used to... ahem... *interesting occurrences* in their bedrooms, and every other room in the house—without her having to give much back to relationship. At least the second type can be broken and re-glued without the fear that you might not exhibit the same sexual prowess as his ex. But, if you're up to the challenge, then good luck, be safe, and don't get a prenup.

This isn't to say that there aren't Aries women out there who take care of their men, rather than the other way around. There are plenty of Aries who bend over backwards to please their men, depending on their moon sign and ascendant. Some people will do anything for love, if they don't think they'll be caught looking weak in front of a crowd. But, do you really want any of the men who took everything without giving anything back?

Aries women are exciting for their partners, volatile in an argument and vicious in their scorn. However, they tend to be at their worst, or best, when they're still with their partner and not after the love affair has ended. They will wait, watch, and plot to see if he will try to come back to them. They store their vengeance until the optimal moment, or they explode randomly any time it looks like the man is either on his way back or gone for good. This doesn't make things exceedingly difficult for you, but it doesn't make things safe either.

She doesn't like you, and the only way to get her to like you is to prove yourself worthy. Every contact you have with her, she will be sitting there, comparing herself to you, finding your faults and your strengths. She will be gloating, bleating niceties, burning inside and wishing to burn you too, or to have you igniting alongside her—with her. It's possible that you'll be doing the same type of comparison, but unless you're a fire sign, you won't be roasting about it like she is. Exploit your strengths, make sure that your man really is done with her, and watch your back.

If There Are Children Involved

The children more than likely won't be with him. Aries mothers are indulgent, if controlling, and they won't let go of their children without a fight. Most men aren't up for the battle, so the kids end up with her. If he does have the kids, then your relationship is almost completely safe because she's resigned control. If she didn't want the kids, or couldn't handle them, then she won't want the father back any more than she wanted to continue being a mother to their children. And, if she's still fighting for the children, she'll be more concerned with getting *them* back than with getting him back—and if he's fighting, he'll be more concerned with seeing that she stays away.

What He Misses

She was a dynamic partner who almost always kept things interesting. She loved and cherished him as long as he did the same for her. Her need for independence and her complete faith that he would always be there were charming to watch. Sometimes. If you like being taken for granted by someone half the time, and adored and clung to the other half.

What He Doesn't Miss

Getting involved with an Aries is very similar to having a toddler around. She's needy, whiny, fussy, and utterly assured that she can do everything on her own. She demands everything—she doesn't ask. And she's utterly unhappy when she doesn't get it, until you distract her with something else. She surrounds herself with ideals and has a lot of difficulty coming to terms with the reality of any situation. She thinks that everyone loves her—she needs everyone to love her, and she lashes out at the smallest sign that they don't.

What You Can Do to Piss Her Off

It's too late for that. You've already pissed her off. The only thing left to do is to make sure that she leaves you and your man alone. Play to your strengths, don't worry about getting off on a bad start with her, and never take your eyes off your man. As with most other signs, you'll need to make sure that he's through with her. And, with fire signs in particular, you have two options of how to proceed: submit or dominate.

How Your Sign Will Handle the Situation

Aries

As a fellow Aries woman, you are more than capable of handling any situation that arises between you and your man's ex. You are fully aware of all her shortcomings, and you know how to exploit her strengths, because, as any self-aware woman does, you know how you would act if you were in her situation. With you, your man will never lack for physical arousal or an able partner... or passion. Just make sure that you don't get more caught up in his problems than you need to. Don't worry that you might remind him of his ex, because all Aries are different enough from one another that each individual one can be a new adventure, not to mention unique.

Taurus

While your man was with the Aries woman, he felt a distinct lack of appreciation. He was her object—he belonged to her and was paraded around by her in front of her friends. You can be the answer to his long-forsaken need for satisfaction and stability. You don't require the continual adoration that so many Aries need in order to survive. You are down-to-earth and reliable. *You* love your man, *you* will protect him, and *you* want the best for him—for *his* sake, or for both of your sakes, but never just to satisfy your own desires. With you, he is home. If things start to get bad with her, you can rely on your quiet, earthy strength to see you through. Fires may burn, but the earth perseveres.

Gemini

You are less physically passionate than the Aries woman was, but you make up for it in intellect and intrigue. In a way, you are more exciting and experimental than the Ram could ever hope to be. However, you tend to pay little attention to the drama going on backstage. You will typically let your man handle the situation—as it is *his* situation, not yours. You are more concerned with your current relationship with him than what his past relationship with her was like. At worst—if he isn't able to control his dealings with her—you will leave quietly, deciding (again, quietly) that he obviously isn't up for a serious love affair with you. Then you will easily find someone who is.

Cancer

The Aries woman was never particularly vulnerable (however, she could definitely be puerile), and she never gave her man the feeling that she needed him—although she seemed to need his reassurance constantly. He will feel as if he holds a real place in your life, and that you not only enjoy having him around, but that you need him there. The worse the situation gets with her, the more your emotions come into play and the more you will feel the impulse to retreat into your shell in order to avoid the assault. Rather than avoiding the issue and letting your emotions be continually hurt, you need to let him know about your feelings early on in the relationship and periodically throughout.

Leo

If the Aries ex is still vying for a position in your man's life, then she will need to accept a seat in the audience rather than a role as a fellow actor, which is something that, as a cardinal sign, she will have difficulty dealing with. You would have no problem with her continued presence as long as she understood and accepted her inferiority. Hopefully, you and the Aries have so much in common (both of you are fire signs, after all) that a friendly rivalry can be established rather than an all-out war of egos. You are just as passionate as she is, but you are more blatantly sexual than she will ever be. And, you are simply a lot more woman. The bright flashes of intense heat he felt when he was with her have been replaced by the steady blaze of a more permanent fire with you. Innocence has been replaced by a knowledgeable embrace.

Virgo

The Virgo and the Aries were just not meant to be around each other in any casual sense. There isn't much about her that you can respect, and the bleating of an upset ram will only annoy you. You are fully aware of her faults, as you have studied them in depth to make sure that you are as unlike her as possible, and you are certain that he is better off without her in his life, period. Yes, she put up with a lot, but so have you, and it's time for her to be on her way. His life with you is more stable, more in control, more productive than it ever was with her. You can show him how to reach his full potential, while she did little besides ride his coat tails and drag him down. She was passionate, but you are steadfast and true. If anyone can withstand Aries anger, it is you.

Libra

You are diplomatic and fair, meaning that you can see her side of a relationship and you know that she was not to blame for *everything* that went wrong. Aries women need to be liked, and the only reason they can understand someone not liking them is if that person is jealous. Your tact will lead you around this problem, and you will be able to appease her without giving up control of your own relationship. Because you are fair and avoid conflict, and she hates being disliked, the two of you are more likely than most to be friends—even if there is an unspoken rivalry between you. As for your new love, he will find your romantic nature at the least charming and at the most intoxicating. The Aries woman has nothing over you when it comes to maintaining a relationship.

Scorpio

What does a woman with a stinger like yours have to fear from a goat? Hooves. If you approach this woman combatively, she will return the favor, and because she knew your man before you did, there is the possibility that she has more ammunition than you do. However, you have the position of power. Even though you won't run from battle, having this woman as a constant presence will take its toll on your new relationship. Try not to seem jealous or biting, as your lover may mistakenly believe that your feelings stem from jealousy rather than a need for emotional security—and if he is the unevolved type of man, he might foster any problems between the two of you in order to boost his own ego. Otherwise, you will survive the rapids.

Sagittarius

Neither you nor the Aries has any qualms about using friendship as a means of revenge. The fact that on any normal day, the two of you would get along and even *enjoy* one another's company just aggravates things. Luckily, you are less passionate about the situation than your Aries buddy is, and vengeance has never really been high on your list of important accomplishments. You are more concerned with the adventures you and your new man are having—all the wonderful places you are seeing and the people the two of you are meeting. Your refusal to dwell on negativity works wonders at this time, and I am certain your man appreciates it.

Capricorn

If you are in a relationship, then you must feel secure with it. You inevitably think in terms of years with your significant other, rather than the hours or days that are the longest measuring sticks some other signs can come up with. The presence of a scorned Aries woman doesn't help stabilize your life, but realistically, it doesn't hurt it very much either. The more women who are after your man, and the more enviable your relationship with him is, the greater the significance of your life together. Right? It's nice to have something that inspires jealousy in others. As a lover, you give your man a sense that anything is possible, and that success is a must. As an enemy, your earthy strength wards off most attacks. You make sure that your life is respectable, so it's hard to find anything to hurt or embarrass you.

Aquarius

The so-called vibrancy of the Aries is little more then cheap glitter to you. You can't see how others are interested in this woman. Yes, she can be "vivacious," but isn't she really just being obnoxious? And, she can also be "seductive," but shouldn't it be called what it is—cheap? You are definitely more credible than she is, and certainly more respectable. Her idealism was nothing more than her inability to handle reality. Your man must agree, because he is with you, and not her. Both you and he know that naiveté is nothing more than a cover-up for ignorance. So, it's settled: she doesn't like you and you don't like her. Now what? Show off your best qualities and leave the Aries far behind you.

Pisces

Your man will find your quiet complacency and intuitive wisdom to be a welcome reprieve from the Aries ego and tantrums. Unlike the Aries, you don't use your men to achieve status, but you do want them to be successful. Be sure to establish yourself as your man's new love interest as early as possible, and make sure that everyone knows how committed you are to each other. An Aries, due to her need for social approval, will rarely fight against a united front. Don't allow yourself to be taken advantage of by anyone, let alone a brawling Aries woman. As a water sign, any confrontation you have with a fire sign should be handled with great care, as the elements of water and fire can destroy each other. Thankfully, you have a great ability to manage confrontations carefully, and you should be more than capable of handling an Aries woman.

The *Taurus* Ex-Girlfriend

Dates: April 21–May 21
Planet: Venus/Pan-Horus
Element: Fixed earth
Representation: Bull

After hearing about what their relationship was like, and dealing with her yourself, you won't be able to understand why it is that many cultures make a sport of taunting bulls rather than leaving them peacefully alone in a pasture somewhere far away. You'll definitely understand the impulse, though. Despite the fact that no one who's getting charged by a bull stops to try to reason with it, this is just what she expects you and your man to do. All of the demands she ever made were secured in her mind as reasonable and rational. That's why she couldn't stand when he'd argue with her about a point she had or try to change her mind about something. "Reason" still doesn't quite explain why she hates red capes, though, and why she lashes out at the slightest provocation—unless she can pass it off as an understandable response to someone tempting her.

Your man's relationship with this earthy Bull was probably a very committed one, as the female Taurus doesn't usually settle for less. Their relationship was full of earthly delights: good food, hiking, art, and physical sensuality. She was a lot of woman, just like a bull is a lot of beef, and unless your man was a china shop, he didn't fare too poorly from his association with the Taurus. Not that he's in perfect shape. (Now would be a good time to make a thorough body check to look for extra holes or puncture wounds where there shouldn't be any.)

She was opinionated, stubborn, and patient in her siege—until she got angry, at which time she'd explode. He could never get the upper hand, as she was notorious for remembering everything he did wrong—a trait that Venus also gives to the Libra. Now that their lovely pairing is broken up, and they are both individuals again, she's still mulling over every fight and criticism while secretly nursing a badly broken heart. If at any time she loved him, she will continue to do so no matter how things ended or what your new relationship with him is like.

You, sweetheart, have nothing to do with it. You barely exist in her world, or in the world that she once considered "theirs." At the most, she will compare their old relationship to the one he has now, wondering why he's changed certain things and laughing when she sees that you're just as annoyed with some of his traits as she was. This does not mean that she will leave you alone. Anyone walking through the pasture of a bull stands the chance of being charged or at the least running into some cow patties. Just be careful that your matador man doesn't use you to distract her from running at him.

She was judgmental and critical of his decisions, and unwilling to discuss them with him on any intellectual or philosophical level. Her earthy groundedness simply never let her brain go more than a few feet above the soil at any given moment. She was mainly concerned with herself and where he fit in her life then the whys and what-ifs of any subject. And, he probably got tired of constantly feeling earthbound. However, she could be very supportive and protective of him when she felt the need or he asked for her understanding.

She wasn't the best of housekeepers, but she controlled their money perfectly and made sure she had a good job with plenty of upward mobility just in case he lost his. Somewhat traditional in her thinking, the female Bull believes that women are best able to control their men if the control comes from the bedroom or kitchen. And it was in these two places, along with the bank, that she excelled in her duties as a significant other. You could best replace her in the areas of intellectual friendship, chess opposition, debates, compromising, and imagination—the areas where Bulls typically do not go. He might not be used to such a woman, but if he left the Taurus lady, one of his reasons was more than likely a deficit on her part in one of these qualities.

If There Are Children Involved

She will be a good, traditional mother. She will try to make allowances for you in their lives, but she won't tolerate her authority being questioned. Tradition and order will be important to her, and she will want you to help carry them out—*if* you have proven yourself to be a constant companion to her ex rather than a fleeting affair.

What He Misses

Her earthy sensuality and wholesomeness. She was a strong, independent woman who still allowed him to have some authority and say in her life. She never leaned on him more than he could support, and she made sure their money went where it needed to. The security he had with her was strong. Even if her temper could be sudden and severe, it rarely showed.

What He Doesn't Miss

The constant fear of being trampled by someone who insists she is being rational eventually wears down any feelings of security and love. Her control of his life always seemed to be an attempt to hide the mistakes she made in her own. After a while she took him for granted. She started to expect things, and she didn't miss the romance of their early affair. Instead she found comfort in the stationary routine of living.

What You Can Do to Piss Her Off

You can wave red flags in her face and tear her bleeding heart further asunder, or you can take the advice given at the beginning of this chapter and leave her alone in her pasture. She will not try to win back your man, unless her moon and ascendant are in a more malleable and violent sign. Be respectable, down-to-earth, and monetarily stable, and she may even like you.

How Your Sign Will Handle the Situation

Aries

Calm, plodding, stable Taurus will be about as exciting as plowing a field in comparison to your seductive heat. While your man might have been quietly dozing during his relationship with the Taurus, you are sure to have him bright-eyed and bushy-tailed in yours. The Taurus woman isn't very interested in you, and you are fine with leaving her grazing in her pasture. Even if she is brokenhearted, even if she wishes every day and night for your man to return to her, you will never know about it—except possibly through gossip. You cannot imagine being as chained to the ground as she is, as...*complacent*. It is unfathomable to you that someone could want something and not try to obtain it. Even if they have no chance of getting it.

Taurus

You are having a difficult time, but it's okay. It's uncomfortable being the rival of a person when you see so many similarities between the two of you. You can understand her need for security, and you're sorry that she didn't find it when she was with your man—but that doesn't mean that *you* can't find it with him. She's just as uncomfortable as you are, and she's probably more confused trying to understand why he is with you when you resemble her so much. The key is in the details. You might exhibit some similar traits, but you are two very different human beings, and your man will not fail to notice the differences. Establish security in your relationship as soon as you can, and then you can worry about the peripherals.

Gemini

You will never understand how your man could handle being continually bored to death by the Taurus. Questions race through your brain about how it started, when it ended, why he dealt with it, etc., but the questions never seem to make it to your vocal chords. Or else, you just weren't paying attention when he gave you answers. Oh well. She doesn't pay much attention to you, but she is secretly jealous of your easy charm and sense of adventure. The impression you give people, the one that says you could walk away from someone at any time seemingly without a backward glance, makes the Taurus's heart start pounding and her blood pressure rise. Your man's heart is pounding too, but for another reason entirely. In layman's terms, you bring a sense of exhilaration to the relationship.

Cancer

Sensuality is a subject that you've never had any trouble understanding, and when it's combined with your ability to make any house or apartment a home, your man is sure to feel loved and well taken care of. There is a possibility that you will never have contact with the Taurus ex, because she is just as likely as you would be to want to be alone while she sulks. And, any contact the two of you do have will be civil, as long as you never lie to her about anything. Both of you understand the value of a good home, so neither of you will try to dislodge the other from your rightful position as wife or mother. Having a Taurus ex-girlfriend around to deal with isn't difficult as long as you don't provoke her into anger. Keep your red cape in the closet and you'll do fine.

Leo

At first you may find it difficult to enter the territory of the Taurus. She is protective of everything that she thinks is hers, and your first job will be to outline what is *actually* hers and what now rightfully belongs to you. This situation that the two of you are in could easily become a pissing contest between the zodiac's two most possessive signs. I know you are up for any battle that comes your way, but your energy would be much better spent on your new lover and not on his ex. You are a more passionate and sexual woman than she ever was, and your fiery attention will enthrall your man. The more enchanted your lover is, the more apt he is to admire and perhaps even worship his new mate.

Virgo

As a fellow earth sign, you agree with the Taurus that home is important. The point of conflict will be about *whose* home is important. According to the Taurus's heart, you are a home wrecker. It doesn't matter how you and your new man got together, and the Taurus doesn't care about what context the term "home wrecker" is usually used in. What matters to the Taurus is the fact that her home was supposed to be stable, and your presence is a symbol that the home she made with your man will never be whole again. You've wrecked it. Therefore, you are a home wrecker. It's simple logic, right? You're not so sure. You see all too clearly how her home was really wrecked, but being a stubborn Bull, she will not thank you for pointing out her mistakes. A word of advice: every time you find something to fault the Taurus for, kiss your man. If you're wearing lipstick, you'll have fun watching his face go from its normal shade to entirely red in a matter of minutes.

Libra

The stubbornness of the female Taurus is incomprehensible to you. You cannot imagine anyone not being swayed by the opposite side of a story, or being unwilling to change their mind when new information comes to light. Well, you needn't imagine it, because the reality is staring you in the face. From experience, your man will warn you about how strong-willed his ex-girlfriend was. He has no idea what strong-willed is, and now that he's with you, he will learn quickly. You, my dear, are a cardinal air sign, whereas the Taurus is a fixed earth sign. And air can wear down even the hardest of stones (usually by picking up and throwing other stones at it). Yes, the Bull knew how to create a loving, comfortable home. So do you. But you can do it with a romantic flair and charm that the Taurus couldn't. Your man, and every man in your life, is sure to be pleased.

Scorpio

You and the Taurus have been in direct opposition to each other from birth, and the situation you now find yourselves in will surely not help anything. Although there is a good chance that she won't hinder your new relationship, you won't be entirely comfortable until she is out of the picture. As a significant other, you are attentive, charming, and supportive. All of these things could also be said about the Bull. However, you add a certain spice to your relationships that the Bull could never give. Your quick wit and agile mind, combined with your explosive sexuality and wisdom, leave little else to ask for in a lover.

Sagittarius

There is something about the Taurus that interests you. You don't particularly care that the two of you are in an awkward situation, in part because you see "awkward situations" as intriguing. You also don't think that the Bull can harm your new relationship or affect your life in any way that you don't want her to, and that helps ease the tension. As a lover, you are much too self-assured to let an ex get in the way of you having fun. The Bull, for her part, doesn't want to be involved in a conflict and will follow your lead when it comes to handling the situation. If you don't wave any red flags, she won't charge. If you respect her and her space, she will respect yours. Mostly. You *will* meet the occasional Taurus who is ready to fight at the slightest provocation, but luckily they are rare.

Capricorn

In any normal setting, the two of you are much more likely to become friends than enemies. Both of you admire success and the benefits of having a structured life. Any tension that arises between you is mostly due to your own thought processes and insecurities rather than anything the Taurus has said or done. Your viewpoint of the situation is key to how things turn out and to the kind of troubles you will actually face. Treat the Taurus with respect, and she will return it in kind. Treat her like a leper, and she will pick a fight with either you or your man. Just remember that your man left her for a reason, but that reason doesn't make her a bad person. And it doesn't make her perfect either.

Aquarius

You can understand wanting peace and tranquility, but this woman is downright boring. You can also sympathize with her need for a secure social position, but you would rather place your bets on achieving a high rank, even if there is a good chance you could lose it almost as soon as you receive it. After spending every night at home with the Bull (they really don't like going out much) or only being around her friends and never his, your man is sure to be overjoyed that he has moved on to a relationship with a woman who knows how to travel the social circles. You can intuit where the best social spots are, and you are a fun and lively date.

Pisces

The feeling of living in a fantasy in which anything is possible will appeal to your man, especially after being with a Bull who has stubbornly stomped him to the ground. The Taurus takes one look at what you and her ex are planning to do with your life together, and she immediately starts critiquing it. This is the exact behavior that helped drive your man away from her. The typical Taurus woman will not confront you about her broken heart, and most Bulls won't even talk to their exes about it—as long as they know that their old relationship really is over. So, you don't have to worry about anything other than your new relationship.

Gemini

The *Gemini* Ex-Girlfriend

Dates: May 22–June 21
Planet: Mercury
Element: Mutable air
Representation: Twins

The first question most people ask about Geminis is whether or not their representation means that they are two-faced. Not only are they two-faced, but they are four-armed, four-legged, and have two rear ends. But they do not appear this way at first. The Twins are identical; their separate lives encompass the same habits and routines. No one is certain as to how the Twins divide, but the universal belief is that they do so unpredictably, and without warning. This is why the Gemini is seen as a fickle, volatile person—apt to change her mind at the slightest whim. Nevertheless, the difference between the Twins lies more in how Geminis perceive themselves—whether or not they attribute likable characteristics to one Twin and negative ones to the other, or if one of their halves is seen as being protective of the weaker other side. The perception leads to a further separation of the halves, thereby making the differences that much greater. Despite the prevalence or lack of a differentiation, the Gemini is still a dual sign, and is therefore more likely to be two people in one rather than a single entity.

Sound confusing? Wait until you meet one. The Gemini woman rarely says exactly what she means (she probably never knows what it is that she *really* means), and while your man was with her, he always felt that according to her, "truth" was only a philosophy to be toyed with and not a reality that could be grasped. As a significant other, she excelled at leaving him off balance. Some men love this aspect of her, but others need a more stable platform. She could be very demonstrative and loving, only to disappear for days without a word. Freedom was all-important to her, and your man was forced to keep out of her way, follow her impulses blindly, or be discarded in favor of a more stimulating companion. And this woman *rarely* lacks a significant other.

Glib and coquettish, she at first appears to be easy to understand and relate to. She swears that she has no interest in hurting your new relationship, which at first you believe. To be honest, it's not that she is going to conspire to doom your relationship. It's more that she's willing to wait and be nice until an opportunity to seize her ex comes up. She'll even give you her number so that if you ever run into any problems, with your man or just with life, you can call her—because she is your *friend*. Uh huh, have fun trying to swallow *that*. She is as much of a friend to you as a car salesman trying to convince you to buy something that will most likely have to be repossessed in a month. Her charm exists for a purpose—to enchant, entice, and enslave, but not to altruistically befriend. Relying on her is as safe as standing on an ice-filled river, each foot on a different sheet of ice, with both threatening to go in opposite directions.

The Gemini woman is known for having a long string of love interests, and chances are that even if your man was more than just a fling, she won't put much effort into getting him back. Geminis are notorious for never finishing anything, and promoting the end of your new relationship is not an exception. As stated above, she will be content to sit back and watch whatever hand fate has dealt you play out on its own, without lifting a finger to do anything about it. However, as Gemini is an air sign, and known for being the communicator of the zodiac, gossip is always a possibility.

Financially, her irresistible enthusiasm for new projects cost him a few dollars and a lot of time, but her inability to finish any of those projects got on his nerves. She can be refreshing and fun, but following her constant changes were dizzying. He'll be happy to find someone more stable, even if that means giving up a little of the excitement.

If There Are Children Involved

She's more likely to be their buddy than the disciplinarian. She'll make sure to do all the fun things with them, leaving the punishment to you and your beau. This is just one reason that they might like her better than they like you. However, because the Gemini represents twins, we must look at the other side of the coin as well. She just might be the authoritarian. If this side of the Twins comes out, then she'll think you and your husband are bad influences on the kids. My advice: pay attention to the legalities of custody and then charm the children while she's off on one of her many tangents. Don't forsake the rules, though.

What He Misses

Her spontaneity, her charm, her zeal for life. She was fun and infuriating, and either nothing could bother her or she'd go crazy over the smallest things. Just when he hadn't seen her for days and he thought they were over, she'd show up at his door or in his bed with rose petals and a brilliant smile.

What He Doesn't Miss

Her unpredictable love and commitment led him to have many sleepless nights, and slowly broke the foundation of trust one piece at a time until there was nothing left. She might come back right now and jump into his arms only to find that he's taken a step to the left at the last moment. He never doubted that others could take his place, and now he's almost glad of it because he doesn't have to worry about her anymore.

What You Can Do to Piss Her Off

Geminis are typically slow to anger, but they can do a variety of unpredictable things once they are mad. The surest and safest way to piss her off is to openly disagree with everything she says. You can also let her know you don't trust her, don't like her, and don't believe her sales pitches. Geminis hate to be distrusted, despite the fact that so much of what they say is hot air. Because the Gemini can go off in any direction at any given moment, it is rare for her to stick around very long when a love affair has ended. The only time a Gemini will stay is if her ex, your new love, is leading her on either for the sake of any children involved or just for himself.

How Your Sign Will Handle the Situation

Aries

You may have thought that you were an independent woman, but you come in a distant second to the Gemini. She has probably already recovered from her breakup, and has already moved on to the next man—leaving both you and your man in stunned silence for a moment or two. What your guy does once that silence is over will determine the rest of your relationship with him. If he gets over the shock quickly and completely, then you can sleep soundly at night. However, if he gets jealous or upset, then your vision of him as the perfect boyfriend/husband will fracture and you will need to make a serious decision as to what to do next. You can offer him more security than the Gemini could, and more attention and consistency. If he knows what's good for him, he'll be more than happy to stay with you without any sideways glances at an ex who has already forgotten his name.

Taurus

I'll start at the heart of the issue (and I could end there too if I wanted, because it's just that simple). You have very little respect for the Gemini. It's hard to respect someone who is constantly moving, exaggerating, and talking. What does she have that's of any real substance? You can understand why her relationship with your man ended—how could it not? And you sympathize with all the trouble he had with the Gemini's lack of commitment, support, and sanity. He will never have any of those problems with you, and he'll be grateful for it. You are down-to-earth and completely stable—nothing like the Gemini.

Gemini

Because the two of you love mental games and are both adept at donning a new personality every week (or at the very least, each of you has two personalities, making your conflict a party of five when your man is included—unless he's a Gemini as well), misunderstandings and manipulation are likely to run rampant in all of your exchanges. Luckily, neither of you can sustain a conflict for long, so whatever issues exist between the two of you will be resolved, forgotten, or ignored before they have the chance to do any extreme damage. And with all of the adventure that you give to your romances, your man will suffer little more than a headache from being surrounded by so many personalities, even if those personalities inhabit only two female bodies.

Cancer

Like the Scorpio and the Pisces, you aren't sure how to respond to the Gemini's independence and waywardness except by shuddering once or twice and then retreating into your shell or swimming into deeper water. When you finally do come out to take a better look at the Gemini, her caustic humor will wound you and send you right back in. Geminis aren't known for their tact, or their stability. Just ask your man how many times the Gemini ventured off without telling him where she was going or what she was doing, or how often she put her foot in her mouth while talking to someone. With you, your man will have a more calm and predictable life. Money and home will be safe and secure, and he will never doubt your love for him. Because of your intense discomfort with the Gemini, your man should be the one to handle any issues that arise.

Leo

The Gemini ex might be waiting for your relationship to fail, but you are confident that she will have to wait a long time. Unlike most other signs, you do not feel insecure about her hanging around. You have the conviction and strength of character to know that there is nothing that anyone, let alone a Gemini, can do to remove you from your throne. As for how you and the Gemini will get along, there is an empathic understanding that you two have for one another. Because of the comfort you feel in your new position as girlfriend, you are free to value the Gemini as a friend, and you can acknowledge her positive qualities without the fear that they will somehow lessen your own. And, because of her passivity, the two of you should be able to establish a comfortable understanding. You are more passionate and sexual than the Gemini was, and any relationship you are in will be filled with raucous laughter and a warm, hearty quality that brings a sense of easy enjoyment.

Virgo

The Gemini fickleness leaves plenty of room for critique when you decide to sit down and think about her old relationship with your new lover. The list of critical mistakes in their past is a long one. First off, she never was a real partner to your man. She barely supported him emotionally, even though she could talk for hours about what she was feeling. Secondly, she could never get the commitment thing down. She tried, though. You, unlike the Gemini, have no problem with commitment, although you do have a tendency to become too committed too fast. You can provide more stability and honest feedback than the Gemini could, and you are a more capable long-term partner.

Libra

Usually, when paired with a Gemini, you are more than willing to overlook (but not ignore) the Gemini's shortcomings. However, you find yourself fixating on them and on the problems she and your man had in their relationship. Everything she does annoys you, and you can't help but wonder what your man ever saw in her anyway. This can become a big problem, as many Librans form insecurities when they dislike their lover's taste in previous women. After all, he chose you, didn't he? What does that say about you? Anyway, once you move past it, and once you remember to forget the Gemini woman, you will be able to put your energy where it needs to be—on your lover. I'm sure he hasn't noticed that your attention has been elsewhere. After all, the Libran charm can work wonders on a man's ego and security. But just think of how happy he'll be once you really are concentrating on him.

Scorpio

The Gemini is a fascinating creature. You can see how the two of you could become friends, if it weren't for the fact that she is your lover's ex. However, as an ex, she is quiet about their old relationship, and she won't try to remind either of you of what it used to be like. She knows and accepts (for the most part) that her man has moved on, and she's probably not even that concerned about it. She has other adventures to take up her time. With that in mind, starting a friendship with a Gemini ex isn't completely out of the question, even for someone who can be as insecure as you can. You have some important things to offer your lovers, the least of which is commitment. You are also more emotional and passionate than the Gemini was, and your man knows that he is needed and wanted in your life.

Sagittarius

You and the Gemini share many traits that should help you build a friendship. However, the Gemini's position leaves her feeling awkward and makes her overly sensitive to any negativity or prejudice coming from you, which can make establishing a friendship tricky. The Gemini has more difficulty than you do with break-ups. Physically, she will walk away and find someone new as quickly as possible, but emotionally, she will dwell in the past for a little while and will always feel somewhat sentimental about her old relationship. This produces the melancholy that you've noted in your interactions with the Gemini. She will *try* to be your friend, and your sensitivity will inspire a certain empathy for the jilted Gemini. As a lover, you are more of a true partner than the Gemini was. She flitted around so much with her opinions and decisions that your man could never count on her for much. With you, he has a friend, a lover, a romantic partner, and a teacher.

Capricorn

If there is one thing that the Capricorn woman can provide for her man that the Gemini could not, it is stability. You are much better at achieving your own success and supporting your man in his search for status than the Gemini ever attempted to be. She could hardly stay in the same country for very long, let alone make a comfortable home with a steady guy—but you can do all that and more, and your beau is certain to appreciate it. If the situation between you and the Gemini starts to get ugly, just remember that Goats have two horns, and that means that there is one for each Twin. The problem is that the Gemini is an air sign, and can quickly flit away if an attack is aimed at her, so you need to be especially careful with your target. However, the Gemini has probably moved on to another relationship, and as this sign rarely holds grudges, she will most likely leave you and your new man alone.

Aquarius

From what you can see, the Gemini lacks any substance, and aside from her intriguing independence and charm, most people simply wouldn't respect her. You understand that she is bright and quick-witted, but her mind is so flighty that you are doubtful about any actual intelligence that she might have. After all, if you have the brains, why not use them? But she never seems to, except when it comes to sales pitches. Luckily, the Gemini won't really be a part of your new relationship, unless your man has decided to keep her as a friend—in which case, she will be a friend, and little more, because the Gemini recognizes a lost cause when she sees one and is too impatient to wait around indefinitely for your relationship to fail.

Pisces

There will always be tension between you and the Gemini, not necessarily because of anything either of you does, but rather because the two of you have been in direct opposition to each other from birth. When your man tells you about his past relationship with the Gemini, your stomach clenches and turns over once or twice because you can't imagine *anyone* being comfortable moving around so much and doing so many things at a time. You are much more emotional and consistent than the two-faced Gemini was, and both of those qualities can be good foundations for a wonderful relationship.

Cancer

The *Cancer* Ex-Girlfriend

Dates: June 22–July 22
Planet: Moon
Element: Cardinal water
Representation: Crab

The moon grants this woman a rounded physique and weepy, emotional ways. She is a very sensitive Crab, and will retreat into her shell anytime the world threatens her. It's not that she can't handle reality; it's that she's never too sure what reality *is*. According to her, it is what can be seen in the varying degrees and dichromatic world of the moon's phases, and not in the keen light of the sun. She is only able to observe clearly that on which she stands—all else is shadowed and magical.

One negative outcome of her constant emotional vulnerability is that she is left open to the development of a variety of complexes: inferiority, superiority, Peter Pan, etc. She is so incapable of understanding reality and thinking of others besides herself, and so sensitive to any real or imagined hurt, that a protective barrier (a shell) will develop to protect her soft innards from the outside world. Call it the Crab Complex. While your man was with her, he was given the job of reinforcing her shell early on, and he's been doing it ever since. She hates conflict, so even during the rough parts of their old relationship, she attempted to keep herself either under control or isolated a good part of the time—ultimately making both herself and her ex dissatisfied with the relationship.

Perhaps because the crab carries its home around on its back, the Cancer is more concerned about comfort than style when decorating her abode. Your man got used to being surrounded by stuff. Lots of it. She is a messy and cluttered individual who tries to keep everything where it is readily available rather than organizing her belongings—a trait found among all the water signs. Housekeeping was never been her strong suit, although she can cook a good meal when she wants to. Her homemaking ideas lean more toward collections and atmosphere—feeling comfortable in her own space and hoping to make others comfortable as well. It's not her fault that she instead makes others feel germaphobic and in desperate need of a shower. If you ever go to her house, it would be a good idea to bring along some antibacterial soap.

Your beau's job as protector of this moon child could be seen in almost all aspects of their relationship. For one, he was her primary source of income. This woman's emotionality, dependence, and hatred of being told what to do tends to keep her out of the workforce—despite her desire for money and the freedom it brings. Secondly, even as an ex, she still clings to him emotionally, and he is blamed for being the cause of many of her moods. Now, after the breakup, she is having more fun with the tragedy of her loss then she had while they were together. She might call him every once in a while, but it won't last for long, as a Crab with emotional damage is more likely to sulk in private than to air her desolation, especially if her ex rebukes her for blaming him for everything. However, a few have been known to enjoy playing the role of a victim, and they will continue to be noisy about their pains. Yes, she can be sweet, romantic, sentimental, and mysterious. These are the better traits that the moon gives her children. But she can also be over-protective, jealous, codependent, and outrageously sensitive.

And how will you fare with this Crab? Due to her tendency to avoid conflict and retreat into her protective shell, she probably won't ever do anything to you outright. But watch out for those pincers, because they can pinch you at the most awkward moment. True, she will avoid conflict with you, but that shouldn't imply that she'll leave him alone. Remember, he was her protector. And her dislike of conflict won't keep her from hurting you either—she'll just do it in a roundabout way.

If There Are Children Involved

The Cancer woman is an attentive mother. She cares for her children as a coach does for her cheerleaders, and she looks to them as a source of attention for herself. She is aware of the often volatile emotions of toddlers and teenagers, and she helps them define their emotional wants and desires, though she doesn't always pay as much attention to their intellectual needs. If she doesn't approve of your new relationship, she won't like you having a place in her children's lives.

What He Misses

Her emotional dependence made him feel needed and loved. Her avoidance of conflict made it easy to take her around many kinds of people without being afraid that she might say something offensive or rude. The essence of the moon gave her a sense of mysterious sensuality.

What He Doesn't Miss

That same emotional dependence made him feel trapped. Her avoidance of conflict kept her from maintaining a job, and suppressed any constructive argument that might have saved their relationship. Her messiness and her emotions made him think that she couldn't control herself or her impulses. An impulsive collector of objects, she spent much of his money on junk.

What You Can Do to Piss Her Off

Because the Crab woman is so private and outwardly conservative in expressing herself, it will be difficult to know how she feels about you. She doesn't necessarily want her ex back, but she doesn't know if she's quite ready to have him gone. A new love affair for her might make her loss easier, but because she idealizes love, the new affair might make her ex look that much more desirable—because he is the "one who got away." The magical shape in the distance is more important to the Cancerian imagination than the gray craters under her feet. The best you can do is to leave her in the dust, and create new dreams and memories with your new man. And, if you can't take her presence anymore, go to your nearest seafood buffet and start cracking open some crab legs—you'll feel a lot better.

How Your Sign Will Handle the Situation

Aries

Your outgoing, argumentative nature immediately puts the Crab on the defensive. She doesn't really like what's going on with you and her ex, but there's little she can do besides retreat into her shell and wait out the storm. Your new man has noticed your nature too, and he finds it exciting to be with a woman who can duel logically with him rather than one who escapes every time the slightest conflict comes her way. This doesn't mean that you are an abrasive girlfriend or wife. Quite the opposite—you love to be romantic and thoughtful and see a smile on your lover's face. Your home will just be slightly more...stimulating...than his home or relationship with the Cancer was.

Taurus

You have a natural affinity for the Cancerian woman. You can understand her need for security and a stable, comfortable home. And, you can imagine how it felt to have her life disrupted by the ending of her relationship with your new man. Yes, you have no trouble empathizing with the Cancer, but that doesn't mean that you will allow her to have free rein in your new relationship. You are very protective of your lover (because you value stability so much), and you never forget just how much damage a rivalry with his ex could cause—especially if it's unnecessary or avoidable. At least there will be little actual negativity between the two of you, and that will help make your new relationship with your man more secure.

Gemini

You find it most displeasing that the Cancer is still deeply attached to her ex. When the three of you happen to run into each other, it is as if you don't exist to her. All she can see is your man. As a free-spirited, rational Gemini, you have trouble understanding how someone can live in such a state of denial. It's almost as if she has no thought but of her own needs, and she exists not in reality, but instead in her own fantasy world—a world where her ex wants her back. Her many emotional phone calls and conversations with your new lover will leave you feeling like he either needs to hang up or you need to leave. It is best if you talk to him about your issues (something you will have little problem doing) and agree to establish some boundaries about his contact with her. Doing so will help, and will bring harmony to your relationship.

Cancer

Both you and the ex-girlfriend have a tendency to dwell on the past. This can be a major area of concern, because she is thinking about her old relationship, and so are you. And, both of you are wondering how it could have gone differently—just what could have happened that would have allowed the relationship to continue. Needless to say, when you are beginning a new relationship, the last thing that you need to do is worry about the ex-girlfriend, but you just can't seem to stop yourself. Both of you are extremely emotionally demanding and insecure, and unless your man sets some boundaries between his new life and his old one, he may start to feel exhausted from the tension. It would be good if you established some boundaries too, and if you made a promise to stop worrying about his past and start concentrating on the future of your partnership.

Leo

You and she could see eye to eye if lions could breathe underwater and crabs could survive in the desert. While it never hurts to try to understand another person's viewpoint, it will take a great deal of effort. Fortunately, there is an easy way for you to deal with the Crab. By giving her space and allowing her to have insecurities and questions, while reinforcing the fact that you are the current girlfriend and that she can only ask for support so many times before you and your man walk away from her, you will help calm her neediness and at the same time protect your new relationship. Everyone around you knows that you are a passionate and protective woman who eagerly defends herself and her loved ones. In leaving the Cancer and starting a new relationship with you, your new man has traded the cool, deceptive ocean for a boisterous and sunny life.

Virgo

Typically, you and the Cancerian female could establish a friendship. However, the place that she held in your man's life leaves you feeling decidedly unsettled. You've already examined all of her mistakes (and his as well, just to be thorough), and because you can see where things went wrong, you are also able to point out what might make them right again. You need to stop doing that—right now. And don't ever do it again. Exes are exes *for a reason*. Your man knows that, or else he wouldn't be in a relationship as highly committed as the one he has with you. Your tendency to critique yourself and everything around you can often make you forget that there is a positive side to everything as well. You have some remarkably good traits—traits that your man is sure to have noticed. Now it's time for *you* to notice them and to leave your lover's past behind.

Libra

At first, the sentimentality of the Cancer will provoke a sense of empathy in you. You understand why she's so upset. After all, her ex-lover is with someone new...someone *better*. But, you are a possessive sign (even if you try to hide it), and you will eventually want her to acknowledge that her ex is better off in his new relationship, and that you rightfully hold the position of his "real" love interest. It's hard to tell whether you will ever get the Cancerian to acquiesce to that, but chances are you won't. She is a very emotional woman, and you will accidentally hurt her (probably many times), eventually causing her to remove herself from the situation entirely. Your new lover will probably be relieved that he is now with a woman who is independent, strong-willed, and vocal about her likes and dislikes. After all, dating a Crab can be a very cold, wet, and painful experience.

Scorpio
It is likely that the two of you will become friends. Even though she is still emotionally wrapped up in her old relationship, and will most likely continue to think about her ex often, she doesn't inspire much jealousy or possessiveness in you. You think that her sentimentality is to be expected, and you give her a certain leeway that you aren't willing to give many others. The two of you have an understanding, and she is likely to be happy rather than jealous when your new relationship succeeds where hers failed. She honestly does want her ex to be happy, and she's glad it's with someone like you. This gives you the freedom to concentrate on your new relationship. Your lover will find you to be

a more intellectual and worldly girlfriend than his ex was, and he will appreciate your quick intellect, your passion and drive, and your willingness to work for your relationship.

Sagittarius

As a Sagittarius, you understand the importance of personal space, of individuality and independence. You know all about accountability. Your new love will have plenty of room to do his own thing, have his own life—and you will be there to support and encourage him. It's a definite change from his old relationship. The Cancer's clinginess could be suffocating, and now that they are over, she is pretty upset, and there's a good chance that she's more codependent on him now than she was before. At first you might try to reassure and defend the hurt Crab. However, once you realize that she chooses to be weak, your patience will run out. There is little chance that you'll get exasperated enough to lash out at her, though it would be a good idea to keep some distance between you and her grasping Crab claws.

Capricorn

Achieving any kind of compromise with the Crab is nearly impossible, as the two of you have had issues with each other from birth. It's not your fault, and it can't be blamed on the Cancer either; you were just not made to get along. The Crab will look to you and her ex for emotional support during the difficult time she's been having since the breakup of their old relationship, and it won't take long for you to get tired of her emotional demands. You will need to remind her that you are not there to support her, and that it is no longer the responsibility of her ex to meet her emotional needs. She will have some trouble accepting her new role, and once she has, she will still feel somewhat sentimental about their old relationship. You are more mature than the Cancer was—a quality your man is bound to appreciate after being entangled in her helplessness for so long. You are also less emotionally driven, less manipulative, and far more successful at work and in the social scene.

Aquarius

Dealing with a Cancer requires a lot of patience and compassion. She demands emotional support, and she still expects her ex to be emotionally attached to her even though their relationship is over. The number of breakdowns he has had to help her through since you and he have been together makes you sick to your stomach. Hopefully, he's taken the initiative and drawn boundaries about how far she can take her neediness, in which case you won't have to deal with her in your life for long. An unfortunate aspect about water signs is that they never seem to truly leave their exes in the past, and they always seem willing to rekindle old flames. Once he is finally through with her, and is able to turn his full attention to you, he will find that you are more interesting intellectually than she ever was, and any house he establishes with you will be of high status and repute.

Pisces

You and the Cancer have a strong chance of friendship or at least of mutual respect. You can understand why she did what she did in her relationship. You can see her side of the story, which is something she will appreciate. You know why she was distant and defensive. After all, aren't you the same way sometimes? There won't be much tension between the two of you as long as you don't misinterpret her quietude as an expression of dislike. Your man will get more excitement from a relationship with you than he did with her. You make him feel that he can be anything he wants to be and do anything he wants to do. He likes that feeling of freedom and possibility. Hopefully he is the type of man who will be grateful that the two of you are on good terms, even if he is a little confused by it.

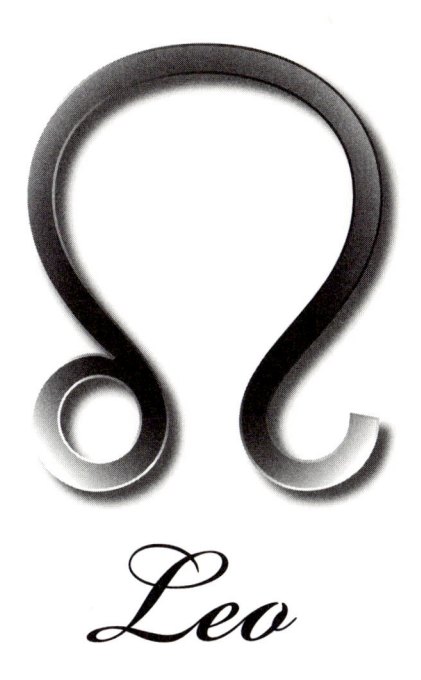

Leo

The *Leo* Ex-Girlfriend

Dates: July 23–August 23
Planet: Sun
Element: Fixed fire
Representation: Lion

The female Leo is, in and of herself, the image of hubris. Her constant drama and bragging will eventually (or so it seems to almost any other sign having to deal with her) bring the wrath of the very gods to smite her. As pleasing a thought that this may be to an Aries or Scorpio (a bolt of lightning streaking across the sky to land square between the Leo's eyes...and boom, she's gone!), a fairer, more rationally minded sign, such as the Libra or Sagittarius, will secretly hope that the gods would *never* give the Leo the satisfaction of a personal smiting. Surely the gods find her as annoying and trivial as you do. Or as you try to. Face it, the Leo is not trivial and never will be. Pathetic, maybe, but not trivial. Her personality just won't let her be something small. She is big—a larger-than-life pain in the ass.

If you are unfortunate enough to find a poor male who has come into close contact with a Leo, you are probably dealing with a man who either has huge ego issues himself or is deeply emotionally scarred from the encounter. The Leo, despite the sign being fixed and not cardinal, is obsessed with dominating everyone in general and her insignificant other in particular. It doesn't matter if the poor boy was already submissive before their relationship. She will find his boundaries and break them further. And then rub his face in the shattered remains of his integrity and individuality.

Here we come to the first question you must ask yourself if you are thinking of starting anything romantic with him: do you really want to help him pick up the pieces? (I'll warn you right now: cat piss stinks and it's hard to fully remove.) If he is the first type of man, the one with ego issues himself, then you also need to realize that you are alone in the clean-up work, because he will never admit to having been hurt, and he will never take your issues with her continued closeness seriously. Oops, did I forget to mention that last part, the one about her *con-*

tinued closeness? Because it doesn't matter if she dumped him; she'll never rest if he's with you. Even if she hated him before you came along, once you've made him smile again, she will need to get him back—to make sure that she's the only one he wants. And she will stop at nothing.

She will call him all the time. Or she will show up at his house when she knows you're not there. Just to talk. I'm sure that if he dated her long enough, he got used to having to help her through some of the turbulence caused by her dramas. He got used to being the shoulder her overly large fluffy cat's head wept on. He got used to rescuing her pride. And if she trained him well, he'll continue to "help" her even when he's supposed to be busy making love to you. What can he say? She needs him. And all the while you're thinking to yourself...yeah, she needs you now, but remember when she locked you out of your own house for three days until you got the point that she'd dumped you? Guys don't usually think like that.

Another thing to take into consideration before you decide to get involved with a man who was the marked territory of a female Lion is that there is a reason that he dated such a bitch. There is a reason that he let himself be dominated. There is a reason that he was eventually dismissed. That reason will continue to be played out as long as he is in contact with the Lioness. He will continue to be submissive to her. It was the way he let himself be trained. Let himself? Yes. A female Leo is domineering, but she is not subtle. If he had any brains, he would've known what she was doing—everyone else did. So, you have a choice here—do you want to be with a man who will always be subservient to his ex?

But...let's stop being realistic and start looking at the situation from the optimist's perspective. Maybe he really is done with her. Maybe he's learned better. Maybe she wasn't such a Leo after all. Maybe he'll stand up to her. If all these things are true, great. You're one of the lucky ones. You've got a good guy. Congrats. Go tell him to get in the shower one last time to make sure the stink of cat piss is gone forever and then go out to see a good movie together—and hope that she isn't there, because then your new beau will have to go home and take another shower later. That's one thing about cats. Once cats get used to urinating in a specific area, they will continue to keep urinating in that area unless all of the previous urine is cleaned up and behavior-modification techniques are set in place to teach the cat better manners. Unfortunately, your man has to be the one to teach her, because she just doesn't give a damn about you.

If There Are Children Involved

She'll be overly protective and demanding. You'll have difficulty making any parental decisions, as she will want to make all of them herself. She may be territorial of her man, but she will be even more so of her children. She is likely to become jealous and defensive if you play any large part in the child's life.

What He Misses

There will be times when he will miss her, when you (as a non-Leo) will fall short of the glittery, passionate, adventurous woman he was with before. Her sexual prowess, although over-blown, was exciting for him. He will miss feeling protected. She made him feel alive and on fire.

What He Doesn't Miss

Although she was a very sexual person, their sex was not always healthy, and if she was displeased, she would make him pay for it. She manipulated and controlled him to the point where she threatened to take his identity away. She was very demanding of his energy, attention, and time. She probably still is. Drama followed wherever she went, and he was often the one cleaning up her messes. Whenever her ego was threatened, it was his ego that sustained the most damage.

What You Can Do to Piss Her Off

Her weakness is her pride. Hurt it in front of everyone she considers a friend and you will cause much damage. Pull her façade apart, but do it honestly so that she can't lie her way out of it and no one will blame you for being spiteful. Public humiliation is key here. Expect her to spread lies and rumors about you and your man, but don't be bothered by it. Everyone knows she's just trying to be catty. That's another aspect that will help you destroy her: everyone knows everything that is going on in a Leo's life because Leos cannot be silent. The only way to avoid a fight with her is to be her subordinate and acknowledge her superiority often and loudly. Good luck, if you have any sense of self-respect.

How Your Sign Will Handle the Situation

Aries

The trouble here is that you are a cardinal sign, and the Leo is a fixed sign who mistakenly believes that she is your superior. Her hot temper and her ego often make her an incorrigible woman, and you just can't help but get caught up in her drama—at least for a little while. (Take a moment to look at the previous sentence and count the number of times I said "her," because *that's* her game, *that's* what she's doing. It's *all* about her.) Your man is relieved to escape an all-encompassing Leo ego. And, while you yourself have been known to have quite an ego, your charming naiveté always helps soften its impact on the people around you.

Taurus

From the very beginning, you and the Leo won't get along. Perhaps it's a leftover instinct from your Bull days, but large predatory cats just aren't allowed to hang around the fringes of the herd. You know that the Leo is waiting ever so stealthily to pounce, and you want to be secure and safe with your new relationship. You can't stand her overly dramatic tendencies, and you deeply disagree with her assertion that she deserves to be worshiped. Your man probably disagreed with it too, and that's one of the many reasons that he is no longer with her. (If he thinks that she *does* deserve the designation of deity, then you and he may not be made for each other.) Even if she is prowling around your new relationship at first, as soon as she meets the business end of a healthy Bull, she'll only attack you from a distance—and you should have no problem deflecting those attacks.

Gemini

There will always be a certain chemistry between the Leo and Gemini that promotes a friendship, no matter what situation they are in when they first meet and no matter what circumstances arise once they have gotten to know each other. The Leo has a certain delicateness that she tries so very hard to hide, and it is usually that small frailty that draws you to her. You know how insecure she is, and how wounded her pride is now that her relationship has ended. You can see her hesitation about what new role she's expected to play, and you want (at first) to reassure her that you don't intend to hurt her. Hopefully she will maintain her boundaries, and you won't have to go back on your assurances. You are actually more adventurous than the Lioness, and you can handle independence and loneliness better than she can.

Cancer

The two of you have issues. It can easily be left at that—I shouldn't have to say anything more, but that would be denying the actual complexity of the problem. First, the Leo likes to believe that she is in charge and you are a subordinate. However, the current situation (and the fact that you are a cardinal sign while she is merely a fixed one) seems to suggest the opposite. Second, a crab and a lion can get in a fight, but in whose domain do they stage the battle—the lion's desert or the crab's ocean? It would be best for all parties to concentrate on themselves rather than their positions. Remember that you have a new man to establish a relationship with, and it doesn't matter what his ex thinks. You are sensuous and sentimental, more softly feminine than the Leo, and you know how to give a man the feeling that he is important.

Leo

When two monarchs are embroiled in warfare, they typically do one of two things: form an alliance and dominate everyone around them, or fight until one of them submits. Either way, the conflict is full of politics and manipulation, not to mention threats and promises. You are more than able to take control of the situation as long as you and your new beau remember the current status of things, rather than the way things used to be. Every Leo is an individual, and you are a separate entity from his ex, despite the similarities that having the same sun sign as her gives you. You shouldn't be confused by your likeness—your man definitely isn't. If you are able to maintain the positive traits that come with being a Lioness (protectiveness, gentleness, caring, and passion, just to name a few), then you will be able to effectively, and maturely, handle the situation you are in. It is the more unevolved type of Lioness who encounters problems.

Virgo

Any man caught between a Leo and Virgo needs to have a large bottle of aspirin on him at all times. That's not to say that he's unhappy in a relationship with you. Quite the opposite. You are a caring and possessive lover who always wants the best for her partner, for his own sake too, not just yours. You aren't hard to get along with if the people around you understand that you have their best interests in mind. On some deeper level, you and the Lioness even have the potential to develop a friendship. But the chances of that deeper level ever being reached are low, because, when it comes to conflicts between the Leo and Virgo, the surface layers are just too thick to get through easily. The trouble is, you can find a number of negative things about the Leo, and the Leo never stops demanding adoration from everyone around her. She'll never get that adoration from you, even if the two of you are able to become friends.

Libra

Anytime someone makes a radical claim, you feel the compulsion to oppose it. This is the characteristic that will first get you in trouble with the Leo. She will grandly claim that everyone loves her, and you will feel the need to point out specific instances where someone hates her. She will dramatically claim that she is *the* star, and you will have to point out the many other stars out there. It's only fair of you to do so, but she won't like it one bit. Your man is happy to be with someone rational, someone who is a true partner rather than someone who pretends to always be onstage alone, with him being nothing more than a prop. Personally, her histrionics send your scales dipping, so it's best if you (and your man) decide to leave the Leo completely alone. Of course, if you have to confront her at any time, your logic and sense of control will either quickly diffuse the Leo's fire or make her explode to such an extent that she embarrasses herself (something that she hates to do).

Scorpio

At first you will be amused by the histrionics of the Lioness. It won't last. You have spent much of your time discovering the realities of the world, and soon you will begin to think it's nothing more than a vulgar show when the Leo (while either speaking in a false accent or wearing a gaudy sequined dress) starts in with her pronouncements and bragging. Then you will become amused by her self-humiliation. As a Scorpio, you feel comfortable pointing out all her shortcomings, even telling her about them while she's in the middle of a particularly long tirade about how everyone needs to respect her. *That* is irony. *That* is amusing. I'm certain she won't agree. Your man is sure to notice the driving intelligence behind your quick tongue, and will be glad that it has replaced the boasting nonsense that he had to put up with while he and the Lioness were together.

Sagittarius

Although you are aware of the Leo's shortcomings, you are more tolerant of her than most other signs are. Perhaps it's because you don't take her ego as a threat to your own, or maybe it's because her boasts are more amusing to you than annoying. Whatever it is, the two of you may actually be able to get along. With your love of personal accountability, you understand that it is up to your man to decide if he is through with her or not. If he is, then you have no reason to worry about her continued presence in your lives. If he's not done with her, that's okay too, because it means that you're done with him, and then it doesn't matter what the Leo is up to. You are a more mature partner for your man than the Leo was, and you are honest, whereas she was inclined to exaggerate. I hope that he is appreciative of what you have to offer.

Capricorn

There isn't much that you find respectable about the Leo, and the fact that she won't leave you and your man alone doesn't help. Your calm assurance can easily deflate the Leo's braggart ways, and if she insists on sticking around, then she will have to learn to either tone down her buoyant personality or face a few pointed remarks aimed at her inflated ego. When it comes to long-term relationships, there's no one like a Capricorn to hold a house, kids, work, school, and love together. Hopefully your man is looking for a permanent lover, because if you have decided to date him (and you care enough about your relationship to be reading a book like this), then you hope that permanence is a strong possibility.

Aquarius

The number of times this woman sets herself up to fall into one of your traps is remarkable. Her ego is the thing that makes it so easy. You are well aware of having an ego yourself, but you are certain that yours is well deserved, whereas hers is just a bunch of hot air and self-delusion. Eventually she will learn to be careful of you, which means that aside from spreading rumors, she will leave you alone. She still might have an attachment to her ex, and instead of fighting with you, she will now try to turn him against you. If your relationship is secure, then you have little to worry about. Your man is with someone who will help him and wants him as more than a litterbox. He is sure to be thankful for your presence in his life.

Pisces

The Leo has an all-encompassing personality, and you may feel an urge to comply with anything she demands. Doing so could leave your man feeling that he is now dating two women instead of one, and while this is a stereotypical male fantasy, don't expect him to be all that pleased about it. Remember, their old relationship was dissolved for a reason—or many reasons, for that matter. You are apt to let the Leo take command because you secretly desire direction. However, you should be seeking it from your new love and not his ex. Your quietude and subtle wisdom are very different from the boastful Lioness, and have a little more truth behind them. You have many qualities that are better than hers, so there's no need to let her trample all over you or your new relationship.

♍

Virgo

The *Virgo* Ex-Girlfriend

Dates: August 23–September 22
Planet: Mercury
Element: Mutable earth
Representation: The Virgin

The female Virgo is the poster child of mental disorders, and she typically seems angry and distant—a temper tantrum waiting to happen. Why is she always so angry? She is confronted on all sides by the imperfections of the world, and she despises imperfection. Somewhere deep inside she's completely aware of all of her own faults as well, which makes the dirtiness and wrongness that she hates so much seem internal as well as external. *That* doesn't make her happy either. She's often cranky, and her perfect Virginity can turn into stale sterility in less time than it takes for a man to lose an erec...um...*interest*.

Typically, when the Virgo is finished with a man, she's just that—finished. That doesn't mean, however, that the man is finished with her. If you run across her out and about somewhere, she will be aloof at the least and rude at most. According to her, she's done with him, and now he's your problem. She doesn't want to be anywhere near him...or you. She's resentful and good at remembering everything she ever had to nag him about. If you want fifty reasons why you should hate him, she'd be glad to tell you. Here, she has the list in her purse.

If your new man has been in a relationship with a Virgin for any length of time, then he has gotten used to being nagged at and controlled. If he was content in that relationship, then he'll have problems with suddenly being forced to think for himself. And, if he wasn't so happy, then you need to watch out for, and attempt to be tolerant of, sudden bursts of independence and selfishness.

In a short synopsis, your guy didn't date a Virgo; he dated his mother. Every little thing in its correct place, every towel folded exactly right, and every piece of clothing color coded and pressed. You'd better hope you're just as good of a housekeeper as he's come to expect his woman to be. I don't mean to say that your man believes in the traditional role of women...but...after dating *his mother* for a while, he might have come to *expect* some things from women. Although he'll mind if his quaint but necessary supper isn't ready on time, he'll be just fine if you don't nag him the way *she* did. He was never so aware of his faults as when he was with that woman.

Cleanliness was all-important to the Virgo girl, and you'd better make sure that you've washed all the nooks and crannies of your body before her ex, your new man, touches you, because he's forgotten that regular women don't naturally smell like apples. And he probably has no idea what a woman without make-up and perfectly shaped hair looks like. The Virgo may be the Virgin, but she was a painted and primped one.

As clean and remote as this girl may appear to be on the outside, she was a boiling vat of emotions inside, and your man probably spent most of his time reassuring and placating his Virgin while they were together. Don't worry, she won't expect him to do it anymore now that he's with you. Maybe. Hopefully. Well. Um. Not because she still calls him, but because he still calls her. No? You'll see. He's gotten good at taking care of this innocent, sweet, conniving, pernicious creature, and it's a hard habit to break. He'll worry about her. He can't help it. She was good at making everyone around worry about her, and if you get close enough, you'll soon know all of her problems too.

If There Are Children Involved

No one takes care of her children the way a mama Virgo does. She knows everything about them, how to control them, how to direct them, how to make sure they grow up correctly. If she's not the one raising them, then according to her they must be absolutely lost to the world. You'll do everything wrong, and her kids will be the ones that will pay, because *you'll* screw them up. "For God's sake, he just spilled milk on the counter and *you* cleaned it up without even yelling at him! He's doomed to become a repeat of his loser father, just you wait and see!"

It can be awful, and I admire your courage, poor girl.

What He Misses

No matter the time of day or night, she was clean, made-up, and smelled wonderfully. All of his needs were taken care of, and she was very concerned with his job and friends.

What He Doesn't Miss

Being "concerned" about his employment and social life meant that she was worried he might fail at everything—after the break-up, the Virgin is now *positive* that he will fail. He didn't succeed at their relationship, did he? If he couldn't even do that one little thing right, he's doomed. And, you're just as doomed because you have the bad taste to date a failure of a man. (A little explanation on the excessive use of the word "doomed": one of the reasons the Virgin is so irate with the world is because she views it as being irrevocably doomed. She's a very negative person, and according to her, there's nothing the world can do to save itself.)

What You Can Do to Piss Her Off

This is a hard one for two reasons: she's already pissed off anyway, and she thinks that you're a loser for dating a loser. No offense to any humanitarians out there, but it is hard to be pissed off at someone who's busy eating *your* leftovers...instead, you sort of just pity them.

At best you can annoy her. Talk about how wonderful a man your new guy is every time she's around. Discuss in detail how successful he is and how well you take of care each other. It won't stop her from being rude. And be careful that your boasts aren't too far from the truth, because she'll be thrilled to point out your exaggerations in front of everyone.

How Your Sign Will Handle the Situation

Aries

It's amazing that the two of you know each other at all, and it's unfortunate that the context in which you two interact has little chance of being a pleasant one. Both of you exhibit similar tendencies, but each of you has a different reason for doing what you do, and that causes most of the friction between the two of you (and is a source of delight for your new love). If the two of you could just openly call a truce, and save your caustic remarks for the private domain, then you'd do fine. Just make sure when you do confide in someone about the trouble you're having with the Virgin, that they don't start spreading rumors. When it comes to your man, you are a real partner and not a parental figure...I'm sure he's enjoying the change of scenery.

Taurus

If having someone critique your every move is acceptable, it is only when that person is someone you love and respect. However, most people never come to love and respect their partner's ex. Being continually judged by a woman your man considered to be unworthy of his time is not on your list of acceptable behaviors. You may hesitate for a moment or two, but sooner or later you will put the Virgo in her place. And, once she's put there, she'll stay there, because a Virgin hates to be embarrassed and you've never been one to be delicate when removing an unwanted influence. At any other time, the two of you would likely become friends, because both of you can appreciate each other's qualities. However, since you are at odds from the start, it would be best if you two just left each other alone.

Gemini

Remember, your man's relationship with the Virgo was more akin to that of a mother and son than a romantic partnership. His relationship with you, however, will be more like an adventurous classical romance than the stable relationship most people expect it to be. Does he mind? Who knows. If he does, you might try for a while to steady yourself into a predictable routine and suppress any out-of-place feelings you have, but it won't last—and neither will he. If he doesn't mind, then the two of you will be sure to run through most of the boundaries that society has ever established and have tremendous fun while you're at it. As for you and the Virgo ex: neither you nor she really puts up with exes, your own or your lover's. And neither of you will hold the ending of a relationship against the other. You two simply don't personalize things quite that way.

Cancer

The Virgo's frigid nature, combined with your own tendency to retreat into a protective shell, leaves little room for any open conflict between you. That doesn't mean that everything will go easily, though. The Virgin has a marked tendency to be overly critical, and you personalize everything to such an extent that you may feel that all her negative remarks are darts and your heart is a bull's-eye. Remember, the Virgin is highly critical by nature, and she has something bad to say about everyone, not just you. Your man never escaped her insults either, and once you've been the victim of a Virgin judgment, you might as well turn to your love and give him a wet kiss because he actually *dated* the woman. Now that he is surrounded by the soothing waters of your cardinal sign, loved and supported in a way that he hasn't been for quite a while, he is sure to be happy.

Leo

Despite the compassion and compatibility that the two of you are capable of experiencing once the external conflict has been resolved, the superficialities of the situation may make it so the deep matters will never get penetrated. On the surface, things are straightforward. You have a tendency to boast, and the Virgo has a tendency to criticize. You don't like her judgment, and the Virgo thinks that your dislike is proof of the accuracy of her evaluation. As you can see, things can get ugly *very* quickly. Because of the tension between the two of you, the Virgo's usual dismissal of her ex might not last; in fact, she might come swinging back into both of your lives. If you don't give her any ammunition against you, and if you are capable of maintaining a respectful distance, then you will never have any problems with her.

Virgo

It is obvious that two such opinionated people will never be able to get along, and will actually spend their time throwing judgments at each other. Being the Virgo you are, however, means that you can see past the obvious, and you've come to your own conclusion about the situation. Both you and she are critical, yes. Both you and she can see what is wrong with each other and with the man between you, yes. However, both of you will usually *agree* about the things you see and the judgments you make. This means that there is a chance for friendship, as long as she doesn't get too critical of your new relationship. Your new lover is sure to feel a little relief that his analytical ex can get along with his analytical new love interest, and the fact that his ex is the same sign as you can make it easier for you to see where she took things too far, and how you can avoid making her mistakes.

Libra

At first the Virgin will try to enroll you in her fan club. She will give you advice, point out all the things in your life that could stand a little improvement, and tell you how you need to rearrange your sock drawer. And, because you are such a pleasant soul, you will attempt to listen respectfully at first and then, later, to show her all the things that you are doing right. Finally, you will shock her by mentioning all of her problems and how she should make some changes. Things may get a little rocky after that. However, the relationship you are beginning with your new love stands to receive only slight damage from your conflict with the Virgo, and most of that comes from your dislike of conflict in general. That's only a small part of the relationship, and most of it will be full of romance and charm—just what your sign is famous for.

Scorpio

While you have been known to wound people, you rarely do it to those who are weaker than you, and in your mind the Virgo is much weaker. There is something about her obsessive need for order that strikes you as frail and insecure. And even when her constant critiques get annoying, you will still have an urge to protect her. To a point. Her ceaseless advice-giving and nit-picking can become tiresome. That's one of the many reasons that your man is glad to be with you and not her. He's sure to find your wisdom and silliness a welcome relief from what he's come to expect from his significant other.

Sagittarius

There is a certain amount of meddling that you can tolerate. Only a *certain* amount. The situation with the Virgo is seriously pushing you into digging up your bow and arrows and playing target practice. Not that you'd ever let her know how you feel.

Your tact will carry you far when dealing with the Virgin. She is full of opinions about your life and her ex, and you don't think that either topic should be open for discussion—after all, she is his *ex*. A few gentle reminders and she should get the picture. She won't stop having opinions, but at least she'll stop telling you what they are.

Capricorn

Many of the Virgo's characteristics that drive other signs crazy don't seem to bother you in the least. You understand her deep-rooted fears, the ones that lead her to be so prudish and demanding. You know that many of the mistakes she made in her relationship with your man were made with the best of intentions. There is a good chance that the two of you will wind up being close friends, despite what your new lover thinks about it. Unlike many other signs, you don't spend much time rehashing your lover's past relationships (unless your ascendant is one of the more possessive signs), so you don't see a need to put up a boundary between yourself and the Virgo. As long as she behaves, so will you. As to your man, he too must let go of past relationships, and his concentration needs to be on the present and future with you, not back there with them.

Aquarius

You shouldn't have many difficulties dealing with the Virgin. There is only one area of concern, and that is her critical judgment of her ex-boyfriend, your new lover. You obviously see something desirable in him, something that makes you want to try to have a good relationship with him. However, she's through with him and is vocal about everything that he's done wrong. You don't appreciate her judgment, and you are more than ready to let her know all the ways in which she failed in her past relationship. If you are able to ignore her, then she will eventually go away. You aren't as much of a homemaker and organizer as she was; instead, you provide your lover with a successful, intelligent companionship. Just because her relationship failed doesn't mean yours will.

Pisces

You can't comprehend how a woman can be so attached to reality when she feels so strongly negative about it. If you don't like something, you avoid it—you don't throw yourself into it slinging insults and judgments behind you as you go. Your only contact with the Virgo will probably be through your ex, or your group of friends and acquaintances, as this woman isn't interested in maintaining friendships after a romantic relationship ends. That's fine with you. She never had anything good to say about you or your man anyway. As for your new relationship, you know how to let a man be a man, and you have no desire to mother him. Your energy is best spent on nurturing your commitment to him rather than building an impossible friendship with his ex, even if you do hate conflict.

Libra

The *Libra* Ex-Girlfriend

Dates: September 23–October 23
Planet: Venus
Element: Cardinal air
Representation: The Scales

The female Libra is judge, jury, and executioner all rolled into one nauseating, dimpled, perfumed box. Like the Leo, she lives to be adored, and her sweetness to you serves one single purpose—to keep her ex around and enthralled with *her*. She learned in youth to keep her friends close and her enemies closer, and she was a marvelous student. One of the most calculating signs out there, she will invite you to lunch and engage you instead in psychological warfare. I warn you now to tread with extreme caution. Never doubt that she's manipulative. Just make sure you catch her in the act before you bring up your reservations to your new lover, her ex one. If you don't, he'll take her side because she's so fluffy and fair-minded. *Of course* she only had the best intentions, and if she slipped up and said something mean, it was only because she's hurt and still upset about their breakup. Why would he feel this way about her? She convinced him while they were together that he was a true man, the only real man she'd ever known (it doesn't matter that she's convinced *every* man she's ever been with of this—your man doesn't realize that), so of course she'll miss him when he's gone. It's only logical to him that she'd want to hurt you, and he probably thinks it's flattering because it obviously means she still wants him. He'll think that you need to show her more compassion, be a little more understanding, try to act nicer...

It's going to drive you insane. Why does everyone seem to love this little hussy with the all-too-ready smile and the quick mind? You can't see it. You don't have the equipment to see it, sister. Sorry.

Like I said earlier, you need to catch her in the act of doing something wrong—the more wrong, the better. She hates confrontation and will be sure to cover her tracks and not engage you in open combat, unless there's a way she can make herself look like the victim and you the aggressor. Hell, at most she'll be distant with you, with maybe a sarcastic comment here and there. Just enough to show your man that you're not worthy, and that she's disappointed with his lack of taste. He'll be compelled to know why and then later, either on the phone or online, but not in person, he will ask her why she disapproves, and if the reasoning is good enough (and with her calculating mind there is a good chance it will be), your relationship with him will never be the same.

As already stated, she will judge you when you meet her for the first time. The judgment doesn't really matter, because either way, if you're acceptable or not, she wants to come first in your man's eyes. If he's been with her long enough, they'll have remained friends after their breakup and he'll miss her. He'll always miss her in one way or another because the manipulative Libran pampered him and boosted his ego so skillfully that he has no idea that anything she told him was something less than honest. You can try to do it too, but it won't be the same as when she did it, and the difference will make it even more apparent to him that you're lacking something. Yes, you. She's messed him up that badly. And now you should ask yourself if you're up to the challenge of forcing him to face reality—to acknowledge that she was not even near to being perfect and that she just manipulated and coddled him. Will he resent you for making him admit that he isn't really that great a guy, that the only reason the Libran told him he was great was to manipulate him? Probably.

If you're one of the lucky ones, she destroyed his pride at the end of their relationship instead of building it up. In that case, he will despise her and you will spend many a night reviewing vengeance schemes with him. Because, the point is, even if he hates her, she's still on his mind. That's just what Libran women do. She finds millions of small ways to become a necessity in his life, ways that he probably won't even see until they are through. If the zodiac has any viruses, the Libran woman would be the top one. Once she sets her eyes on a man, she usually gets him, and it takes a strong dose of something... anything... to make her go away.

If There Are Children Involved

She will be concerned with your ability to raise her kids. She is a protective mother, and any corporal punishment by you or her ex will be strongly questioned by her. She will be more concerned about your ability as a parent than you taking her place, and any problems her children have in school will be blamed on you.

What He Misses

She made him feel good about himself. She carefully removed any insecurity he had. He'll miss that rational way her mind worked, how she noticed things that no one else did. She made him proud to show her off. She was a true friend to him and took his side more often than not. She was fair and diplomatic and she always tried to avoid fighting.

What He Doesn't Miss

Her fluctuating moods and her manipulations. Somehow he was always the bad guy, and her calculated use of logic made her hard to argue with. She was most likely conservative about her opinions and sex, although she'd talk about both readily enough. She never could make a decision about anything—half the time. The rest of the time she was domineering and impatient.

What You Can Do to Piss Her Off

Libra is the sign of partnerships, and if you threaten her with the loss of her relationships—romantic or platonic—you will drive her into a frenzy of anxiety. A warning, though: never do anything for which she can blame you, because she will use it against you at some point. Librans have a keen sense of fairness, and if you appeal to her as a friend, and become more of a friend to her than your beau is, then she will be more protective of you than she is of him.

How Your Sign Will Handle the Situation

Aries

Despite Libra being the sign of relationships, you are more likely to be true to your partner than she is. Even if a Libra is in love, she will only rarely feel passionately about it, whereas you feel passionately about *everything*. Astrologically speaking, both of you are opposites and your personalities tend to complement each other. What this means to your relationship is this: your man was either really sick of the Libra and is positively giggling because he's so excited to be with you, or he wishes you had a couple of the Libran's traits. My advice to you is to just be you and let him either adore you or leave. If he decides to stay and love you, then you have nothing to worry about from the Libran. Either way, you'll be fine.

Taurus

The soft-spoken and yet vibrant Libran female is tactful enough to calm your immediately defensive nature. She assures you that your place is secure, all the while winking and smiling at her ex. You don't like it, but her flirtatiousness is never quite enough for you to feel the need to do something about it. After all, she's flirting with you (and everyone else in the room) as much as she is with him, and you find her constant reassurance soothing. If your man was with her for any length of time, he is well versed in the Libran's charm, and chances are he won't fall for it again. Even though Libra is the sign of marriage, you are actually better at committed partnerships than she is. When all is said and done, your man is sure to find the stability you provide a welcome change from the coquettish Libra.

Gemini

It's true that you and the Libra have many traits in common, but that doesn't mean that your similarities will bring the two of you together. For instance, both of you talk...a lot. In many cases, the two of you could enjoy hours of conversation. However, both of you also hate conflict, and the situation the both of you are in is ripe with issues. So, most of the talking that is going on is not to each other. Most of it is what others call gossiping. And in the long run, this can lead to a confrontation worse than if the two of you spoke about your issues to one another. For a time, your man could feel caught in the middle of a very witty and sarcastic battle, but once you have worked things out with the Libra (which you will do, eventually), then he will be happy to have traded up for a much more charming and adventurous partner.

Cancer

After dealing with the conflict between the two of you for some time, you will start to believe that Librans have two dishes on their scales not to be able to weigh things properly, but so you can grab one in each claw and pull the damn thing out of her reach. Being balanced and fair is the basis of her egoism, and she uses her scales as a defense against insults. For example, if you try to tell her she's being unfair, she will just placidly point at the scales and show you how what she's doing is perfectly fair. At first, she will come to you under the guise of friendship, claiming that she holds no grudges against her ex or against you. It won't take long for you to notice how gently manipulative she is, but once you do, you will get out your claws and...ouch. The Libran has forgotten one important fact about you: Cancer is a cardinal sign too, and that means that you don't appreciate being told what to do or being treated like an invalid.

Leo

At first you are charmed by the Libran lady. She seems nice. She seems compassionate and she listens to your concerns with a tactful air. It won't take long before you reverse your opinion. Soon you will start to notice the bossiness of Libra, and that she is more than willing to use all of those conversations that the two of you had to her advantage. She doesn't like you; she only tolerates you, and that means that she has no need to protect you. Instead, she will manipulate her way into your life, and then she will start trying to control things either by being the leader or by wanting to rescue your new man from his relationship with you. Both you and she enjoy being the center of attention, and neither really likes to share the spotlight. This can cause numerous difficulties in both your private and social lives.

However, your passion and ambition are sure to consume your new relationship, leaving no room for a Libran influence.

Virgo

Perhaps because the Libran seems so nice, so tactful and pleasant, you have the desire to help her. It never occurs to you to ask if she needs help, because you are so acute at analyzing people that you *know* she needs help, and you know exactly what she needs help with. However, the Libran doesn't react well to your efforts. In fact, she will eventually lash out, leaving you confused and hurt that your good intentions have been turned against you. On a positive note, the situation will just further your understanding of what went wrong in her relationship with her ex. You know that she was supportive of him, but she was probably *too* supportive. In fact, she was downright enabling. He doesn't have to worry about that with you. You'll keep him in line, praise him when he's done well, and help him figure out how to solve his problems. He'll be a better man for having been with you.

Libra

When two Librans square off in conflict, there is no need to worry about the chance of an actual confrontation taking place.

Both of you balk at the prospect of yelling at an adversary and getting yelled at back, let alone facing the possibility of a physical assault. At worst, the two of you will either ignore each other or sling weak insults in each other's general direction. Passive aggression will take the place of any honest resolution to the problem. Both of you talk constantly, so it is to be expected that rumors will abound. As with any same-sign conflict, you have the chance to discover what areas she failed in, and because the two of you are alike, you can learn from her mistakes and make sure that your new relationship doesn't follow the same path that hers did. I'm sure you will do well. After all, relationships are your specialty.

Scorpio

There are certain aspects of a Libran that you have little tolerance for. In the same way that an ex-smoker can be overly critical and demanding of current smokers, you lack a certain sympathy for the Libran lady. So much of her is superficial, and she has a dislike for anything too involved or too strenuous, whereas you live for passionate pursuits of philosophy, science, or psychology. However, in other areas such as the need for love and reassurance, you can understand and empathize with the Libra. You know that it hurt when her relationship ended, and you know that her pride has been damaged, and instead of exploiting the weakness, you almost feel a need to protect the Libran—as long as she doesn't get too close to your new lover. She senses your compassion and your desire to help her move past the superficialities of love and into the deeper truths of the world in general.

Sagittarius

Both you and the Libran avoid conflict, so there is a good chance that no actual confrontation will take place. You often use friendship as a guise to keep close tabs on your enemies, and the Libran uses friendship as a way to gain admirers. As long as you don't mind her flirtatious nature, and you let her bat her eyelashes at your new lover once in a while, the two of you will do fine. Besides, even if an ex does come back to the Libran in hopes of rekindling an old flame, the Libran rarely agrees to give it a try. She's all hot air with no delivery when it comes to flirting. Even though the Sag is not known for her willingness to commit, you have a deeper understanding of emotions than the Libran does. After all, you are a fire sign, a sign of passion and desire. And your relationships have an authenticity that hers lack.

Capricorn

Because you require stability before entering into a relationship, and the Libran is never that interested in causing problems with her ex's new girlfriend, the only issues that the two of you have are differences of opinion and personality. Although the Libra represents marriage and partnerships in the zodiac, she isn't known for committing herself to a single man for the long term. You, however, know what kind of man you are looking for (and you have known since birth). And once you are in a relationship, it has a good chance of being a permanent one. Your ideals, opinions, desires, and all-around personality are all far more stable than the Libran's. There are certain traits of hers that you admire, but when it comes down to it, you can see why she and your beau broke up.

Aquarius

The Libran lacks any backbone, and her difficulty making decisions can be used to your advantage. Yes, she will always try to keep an ex-boyfriend around as a current devotee, but you are more than willing to set up a strong protective barrier around your new relationship. And you might even use her charming and seductive ways as a means of testing the strength of your new relationship. If your man passes the test, then he will finally be rid of a woman who does little more than charm her peers and collect romantic admirers. You know how to climb the social and business ladders, and you will make sure your man does something admirable with his life. Intellectually, you will take him to new places, and both of you will have conversations that he could never dream of having with a Libran. Yes, she was bright, but you are so much more...

Pisces

Libra is the sign of partnerships, and you are the sign of the truth behind theories. On some level you can see beyond the Libran's façade of gentleness and balance, but on another level you are completely confused about why she does what she does. This half-understanding can cause many misunderstandings between the two of you, and if there is anything that both the Libra and the Pisces hate, it is to be misunderstood. So, the chance for friendship is slim; however, both of you are fully capable of maintaining a healthy ambivalent acquaintanceship. Your own far-out dreams and intense philosophical mindset will leave your new man feeling that the possibilities of your relationship are endless. And, your neediness will make him feel wanted, whereas the Libran independence made him feel like little more than a sidekick.

Scorpio

The *Scorpio* Ex-Girlfriend

Dates: October 24–November 22
Planet: Pluto
Element: Fixed water
Representation: Scorpion

Scorpio is the second and last of the signs with pincers. Unlike the Crab, the Scorpio has a stinging tail and poison to go along with the claws. A Scorpio woman is perhaps the hardest of all the signs to deal with because vengeance and obsession characterize her relationships. She never takes an injury without hurting her opponent, and she was always convinced that her man would leave her for another woman—and your presence has vindicated her paranoia. She will not take this insult lightly, and you can very well imagine that a large target has been painted on both your and your man's foreheads.

Secretive and misleading, she fears that all others will take on her personality and attempt to keep secrets from her or lie to her. The greatest fear in an emotional, self-centered mind is that the worst traits exhibited by oneself will be prevalent in others as well. The Scorpio is fully aware of her own malicious deeds and thoughts, and rather than cleansing herself of them, she will defend herself by finding fault in everyone around her. "If they can be mean, I can be meaner" is her personal motto. In all of the zodiac, she is the best reason to invest in pesticides and insecticides. One reason she distrusts others is because of her strange habit of outwardly acting one way while inside she is a calculating observer, preparing for all contingencies. Ultimately, she is afraid that everyone else is doing the same thing.

If your man has been unfortunate enough to come into close contact with a Scorpio, he was probably in over his head immediately and had to struggle to extricate himself from her lair. She can be a captivating woman, quite sexual and unpredictable. At first he thought she was exciting, but by now he has realized his mistake. She is exciting *and dangerous*. So many signs out there wish to believe that they are dangerous—the Leo and Aries, for example—but none have the flair of a spiteful Scorpio woman. At first she is enticing, flirtatious, and sexually demanding. It's not until later that she begins to secretly stalk him, her fear and possessiveness taking control once again. And here we come to a contradiction in her basic personality—she can be both jealous and dismissive at the same time. There is little stability to be found in a relationship with a Scorpio unless she is assured that her man will never leave her. And, well...your man did leave her, didn't he? Even if she broke up with him, his turning to someone new is a sign of disrespect, a validation of one of her worst fears, and must be atoned for. You are going to have a very difficult time, my dear.

The Scorpion's planet is Pluto, the God of the Underworld in mythology. The Scorpio's soul investigates the dark secrets of life and death, the beginning and end of everything. In a first fear of death, the Scorpio woman learned to grasp at what she wants and cling to it for fear that with death will come loss. And loss is not something a Scorpio is prepared to handle, so she tries to control it. As she matures, every pain and humiliation she endured in childhood and afterward is used as validation for her need to control others now—to hurt them when they hurt her, to toss them aside before they can leave, and to do anything in order to protect herself. She will let you know when she is through with you, and not the other way around. So, if she didn't cut the line between her and your beau, then you can expect her to be involved in your relationship until she's finally ready to let him go.

When facing the unavoidable onslaught, you might hope that some protector (your man?) will swoop from the skies and carry you away from the vile beast that assails you. Here is where the harsh philosophy of Darwin comes into play. Survival of the fittest, my dear, not of the nicest or the prettiest. But do not engage in obvious warfare; be secretive and defensive instead. Anything that you attack her with will be seen as a call to arms, and she will gather her friends to help her in her attempt to "defend" herself. Don't give her any excuse to insult you other than the obvious one of having taken her man. A special caution is needed for anyone dealing with a potentially explosive Scorpio lady: the powers of Pluto give this woman the ability to see through people. If you are insincere, or foolishly attempt to manipulate her, she may simply reject you, but most likely there will be some act of vengeance.

If There Are Children Involved

A Scorpio mother is possessive and overly protective of her children. She can be either a troublemaking playmate or a strict and remote disciplinarian at random. She will not appreciate having you in the children's lives, and she will do what she can to see that they don't like you. She is not beyond gossip and rumor-spreading, even when talking to her own kids about their new stepmom.

What He Misses

Dating a Scorpio is a perilous journey, most often taken by masochists or aspiring heroes. He misses the excitement and sensual exploration that came with their old relationship. Her jealousy made him feel desirable and attractive.

What He Doesn't Miss

Constantly being punished for any real or perceived slight got wearisome, especially when the punishments outnumbered the rewards. He was late from work...*sting*...he didn't say thank you...*sting*...he looked at another woman who just so happened to be walking by...*sting*...he forgot to tell her who he was on the phone with before dinner...*sting*...he went out to a bar with some buddies...*sting*...he has a female boss...*sting*...It just wasn't fun, and he completely forgot who was supposed to be poking whom in this relationship. He didn't like her continual distrust of him, as he always felt like he was having to defend himself. She wasn't always a generous lover; in fact, she could be cruelly sarcastic and indifferent.

What You Can Do to Piss Her Off

Do you really want to do that? As tempting as it may be to get your revenge for all of the things she has done and said against you, this is one war that you'd be better off avoiding. The only way to truly avoid conflict is to become her friend, and even friends aren't immune from her sarcasm and jealousy. Becoming friends with you just might hurt her ex, your new man, and that's a thought that appeals to her. Remember, friendship works two ways, with both people having their own motives and desired ends.

How Your Sign Will Handle the Situation

Aries

The Scorpio woman is particularly dangerous to you. The reason for this is that water puts out fire, and the Scorpio is a lot of water. She is wise and logical, strategic and outwardly calm, but also vindictive and hurtful, spiteful and cunning. Your exuberant and playful nature is not prepared for this type of assault. To win against a Scorpio requires hours of thought and planning, and that's just so... tedious. You'd rather have it over with *now*. Draw firm boundaries and maintain them. I'm sure your man will appreciate you aiding in his escape from the jealous Scorpion. Always remember (for good or ill) that Aries is the god of war.

Taurus

Scorpions are devilishly fast creatures, and they escape easily from being trampled by hooves, but before you decide to start a stampede, remember that you are bigger and tougher than a Scorpio. Nature never meant for you and the Scorpio to be friends. In fact, the two of you have been in direct opposition to each other from birth, and the resulting tension doesn't make any affiliation easy, let alone the triangle that you are in now with her and your new lover. She's jealous and emotionally demanding, and both of those characteristics send you into the defense of your new relationship. Their old relationship is over; now she just needs to realize it. You are the one who can provide a healthy home life and a commitment for your lover.

Gemini

When a man is used to a clingy and spiteful lover who demands attention and submission, he often gets confused if he later becomes involved with a Gemini, even if at first he isn't sure what to make of you. He will revel in your independent nature, and enjoy the many adventures you take him on (unless he is an earth or water sign, in which case he won't know exactly what to do with you; he'll just know that he wants you). You will not only let him have fun with his friends, but you may even join him in his escapades. You are anything but needy (except for a few of you who are known for codependency), and when a lover leaves you, you may pine for a moment or two, but you will quickly move on to the next adventure. While you might be intrigued by the Scorpion, you will never allow yourself to get close enough to be stung by her. You know which end is her business end, and your glib charm and unpredictability will help you avoid it.

Cancer

You and the Scorpion have much in common, but when it comes to relationships, you are less vicious than she can be, and you would much rather have a stable home life than the constant drama that seems to follow the Scorpio wherever she goes. While the Scorpion is usually willing to sting anything that comes her way if it looks like a threat, for some reason she only rarely makes a stab at you. There seems to be a certain understanding between the two of you: you know that you have little to fear from her, and she isn't as upset that her ex is with you as she would be if he was with someone else. The two of you, if either had the inclination, could actually become good friends.

Leo

The stinging, merciless judgment of a Scorpion can leave you feeling as though you just walked into the United States Supreme Court with nothing on. She makes you uncomfortable, to say the least. However, you intuit that behind her deadly sarcasm is a myriad of doubts, and once you understand that, her ability to scare you diminishes. You need to be comfortable in your new relationship, and it would be best if you could focus your attention on your lover rather than constantly trying to protect the both of you from his ex. My advice: get out of the reach of her stinger, and stay out of reach. Both you and the Scorpion are passionate lovers, but you have a warmth about you that makes men feel at ease. She is jealous, whereas you are protective, and your confidence strengthens you while hers is a mask.

Virgo

Despite the pointed quality that all Scorpios possess, you can't help but feel an affinity for her. You don't quite understand why, but even with the position you have in this situation, the Scorpio appears to be protective of you, and this can help mend some of the issues that you are dealing with. There is little actual tension between you that is caused by the situation both of you are in. The Scorpio, although extremely vindictive with other signs, hesitates to act like that with you. Perhaps she senses that there is little she can do to a woman who is so organized and circumspect. Or maybe it's because somewhere in her wizened soul, she senses that you do care for her ex, and with whatever love she has for him that is still within her heart, she honestly wishes him happiness.

Libra

The Scorpio is everything that makes you feel uncomfortable all wrapped into a single human being. She is spiteful, jealous, suspicious, demanding, malicious, and driven by emotion. Even at the best of times, the fact that you are in the same proximity makes you double-check that your doors are locked at night. She knew that her man would leave her. She knew he wasn't faithful. And she knew that he'd rather be with a gullible dingbat than with her. She isn't afraid of hurting your feelings, and will go out of her way to make you feel insecure about your relationship, often resorting to public embarrassment, blatant harassment, and even stalking. Your man, I'm sure, is glad to be out of the reach of the Scorpion lady. As a girlfriend, you are gentle and supportive, whereas she was possessive and paranoid. The relationship he creates with you is sure to be built on a foundation of mutual respect and trust.

Scorpio

It is an astrological fact that the only sign capable of handling a vengeful Scorpio is another Scorpio. The two of you can get into a fight and sting each other as many times as you want to, and your hard shells will provide defense while your tails go on the offense. The truth of this "fact" depends on the individual. Many Scorpios get hurt easily, which is why they are so jealous and possessive. When they love something, they really love it, and it hurts when that something runs away. You can sympathize with the Scorpion's pain; however, you won't tolerate her continued presence in your new relationship. Both of you can be vindictive, so you will be able to anticipate most of what she does to hurt you or your relationship. That doesn't mean that it will be easy having a fellow Scorpio as an adversary. Even if you are good at anticipating her moves, having to protect yourself twenty-four hours a day, seven days a week can get tiresome.

Sagittarius

Despite the fact that the Scorpio is a water sign, that Scorpion always seems to have a little more fire in her than is necessary or comfortable. With other signs, the Scorpion's fire is usually not tolerated, and even sometimes despised; however, you see little threat in her, which makes it easier for you to calm her vengefulness and avoid her stinger. As an actual fire sign, you can see the inferno raging in a Scorpio, and you understand how it burns not only those around her, but herself as well. You aren't as possessive as the Scorpion lady, and when your relationships end, you spend more time intellectualizing the event then grieving the loss of a lover and friend. Because of your understanding, empathy, and passivity, you won't have many problems with the Scorpio as long as your man is through with her. There are plenty of interesting and amusing Sagittarian traits that should more than occupy his time.

Capricorn

Unlike the Scorpion woman, who craves power but is riddled by secret doubts and paranoia, you are able to solidly achieve success, and with it, authority, and you will only be truly happy once you have secured that authority—and you *will* secure it. The way that the Scorpio handled her past relationship is similar to the way she handles power—by being terrified that she will lose what she has fought so hard to attain (and it's through this jealous possessiveness that she usually loses relationships). You are more emotionally detached than the Scorpion could ever be, and any relationship you enter into will be stable, or it will be dissolved. Because of your solidity and confidence, you have a much better chance *statistically* of your relationship succeeding than she did.

Aquarius

With the amount of tension between you and the Scorpio, it is amazing that the two of you haven't imploded or started the third world war. You were simply never supposed to be around each other, and it's an astrological and fateful goof-up that you are in the situation you're in. Both of you are highly suspicious and nervous creatures, each of you hold secret doubts about your own abilities, and both are willing to use any weakness you can find against each other. Can you see how this might be a little messy? If the Scorpio's stinger is relentless in its attack against you, and it feels as if she is never going to leave you alone, then the two of you have taken things too far. Remember, the conflict between you is due to a broken relationship that you weren't in. The Scorpio needs to move on, and you need to concentrate on your new lover.

Pisces

At first you may feel as though the Scorpio has many positive qualities that could result in a later friendship. However, you will soon learn that Scorpios have two sides: one is their logical, philosophical head and the other is a vindictive stinger. The Scorpio is so jealous and has a tendency to be so petty that you get annoyed with her fairly easily. You can understand why she is upset, but that doesn't mean you are willing to deal with it for any extended length of time. Your man will soon find how mellow and dreamy you are, and I'm sure he will be glad that you lack the offensiveness of his ex.

Sagittarius

The *Sagittarius* Ex-Girlfriend

Dates: November 23–December 21
Planet: Jupiter
Element: Mutable fire
Representation: Centaur, also the Archer

Sags are the true humanitarians of the zodiac, even though many astrologers give the title to the Pisces. As a humanitarian, she pities you for getting stuck with such an arrogant, lifeless, stubborn, stagnant man. She too once fell into his trap, but she has since learned better and hopes that you will learn from her mistakes rather than repeat them yourself. However, if she doesn't really like you, then she might just think that you and he deserve one another and wish you both the best (or in honesty, the worst) of luck. And, whether or not she likes you, it doesn't mean that she'll just leave you two to your fates. You don't get off that easily, sweetie. The Sagittarius might not be as vicious as a Scorpio, but her representation is the Archer—which means this woman comes fully loaded. She isn't mean in her attacks, but her gentleness shouldn't imply that her abuse is pain-free.

Typically, this woman is fun-loving and carefree. She is constantly on the go, either mentally or geographically, and while they were together, your man probably accompanied her on many of her journeys—when he was invited. Sometimes, this wandering lady preferred to be on her own, and probably didn't tell him everything that she was doing while she was gone. Even if she hadn't been up to any misdeeds, her lack of disclosure may have lead your man to feel suspicious and distrustful—damaging the security of their relationship.

Despite her assurances (if she was willing to give him any), it's natural that he started to wonder where it was that she actually went. The Centaur woman doesn't like to be restricted, and will balk at what she sees as any attempt to restrain her adventures. This peculiar form of self-centeredness on her part can really damage a man's ego. By the time you've finally started to make those hoof prints on his backside go away and pulled out all the arrows, he will probably still be unsure of women in general—the Sag taught him that he should never rely too much on a woman. Where exactly did she go? With the Sagittarius, no one really knows. Unfortunately for him, she *is* known for having many lovers, and it's not *that* unlikely that she was with one of them. Her insistence on freedom can lead her to try a man's patience and weaken his trust—often breaking it.

Despite her willfulness, she is an interesting intellectual and physical companion. She is more of a friend to her lovers than a passionate romantic interest, and the Centaurian woman is not known to be overly demonstrative when in love. She actually *does* know how to be romantic, but only rarely feels any inclination to do so. The reason is that she cannot stand the clinginess that comes with some men's affection, and the definition of "relationship" oftentimes appears to her to be the same as the definition for "constriction." The Centaur cannot stand to be constricted in any way, and romance is often seen as a precursor to, or the cementation of, a relationship.

Now that they are apart, she will try at first to maintain a friendship with him for the sake of sentimentality and self-esteem. But, as time goes on and the memory of the relationship retreats, she will be content to leave him behind as well. Before the memory fades, she will not be against having an affair with him, even if he is with you. She may even try to befriend you in an attempt to get closer to him. How could this supposed humanitarian be so catty? She believes that you are his responsibility, and if he is willing to sleep with her while he is in a relationship with you, then you'd be better off without him anyway. A real humanitarian perspective, huh?

If There Are Children Involved

The Sagittarius mother is a tolerant woman who seeks to befriend her children. Sagittarians love laws and religion, and occasionally you will find one who is more interested in upholding her own beliefs than in doing what is best for her children. Having children with a man doesn't secure her attachment to him, either financially or emotionally. She won't mind if you are in the kids' lives, just as long as you don't try to uproot her influence or change their religion.

What He Misses

The sense of freedom and acceptance that emanates from this woman is intoxicating. The no-strings-attached attitude gave their lovemaking a sense of abandon, which he will always remember fondly. She was a true friend and companion, with always something interesting to say.

What He Doesn't Miss

The lack of emotional attachment left him without the ability to get more from their relationship. He was never quite sure of how attached to him she was, or when she would take off on yet another unplanned trip. Her cold, calculating approach to love caused him to wonder if he was just another acquired object, meant to decorate the room and provide stability, rather than a loved partner.

What You Can Do to Piss Her Off

There's not much you can do. She has her own circle of friends, her own life, her own ambitions, and you just don't fit in her plans. She's not one to dwell on what-ifs, and when she and your man broke things off, she hardly spent much time wishing they were still together. She's not jealous of you, and you don't have anything that she wants or couldn't get for herself. It's best if you leave her as she has left you, and hope that your man can do the same. If, however, she attempts to befriend you, make sure that she isn't using you instead.

How Your Sign Will Handle the Situation

Aries

Once upon a time, in a land far away, the two of you could have been best friends. You have many similarities, one of which is having a sense of fun. Both of you are idealistic and optimistic; however, you are also on opposite sides of the war in this situation. Despite the touchy circumstances, you have an urge to identify with the ex-girlfriend (after all, the two of you are very alike), which your new man might find a little disconcerting. You can offer your beau more passion and commitment than the Centaur could, and you are less of a psychological game player than she was. Make sure you remember that you are here for *him*, and not to be the judge of what his old relationship was like. That way you can maintain a boundary between you and his ex while keeping your new relationship intact.

Taurus

You find the joyful antics of the Sagittarius to be charming and entertaining. You love to watch her work, and because she doesn't appear to be treading on your new relationship, you won't feel any need to defend it from her. However, just because that is how things appear on the outside doesn't mean that she *isn't* trying to disrupt things in your life. Remember, the Sag often uses friendship as a way to break up a relationship. If you're lucky, then the Sag honestly does like you (and this isn't such a far stretch), and she will eventually forget about her ex-boyfriend and her original intentions for befriending you (asking the Sag to forget something isn't such a stretch either) and will become a true friend. When it comes to your new lover, he's likely to find his relationship with you to be more satisfying and secure than his relationship with her was. You have such a soft, seductive quality about you that many men are happier lying in bed with you, in a home the two of you have built together, than taking the next plane to Paris just because the Sag had a whim to do so.

Gemini

Both you and the Sagittarius have a love of travel, adventure, and communication. There is a good chance that the two of you (or the four of you, as you are both dual signs) will become friends and even establish a greater rapport than you have with your current beau. One of the challenges of admiring your man's ex is that you may have difficulty understanding why they ever broke up, and you need to work on accepting the reasons for the breakup that your man gives you. This is made especially difficult because the Sag is known for using friendship as a way to rekindle old flames, and with such a likelihood for friendship that you and the Sag have, it will be difficult to see through her manipulations, which could leave you feeling more than a little used. As a girlfriend, you are more committed than the Sagittarian, and you will be more willing to take your man along on your adventures than she was. Also, you are pickier about who you date than the Centaur was, meaning that there is a good chance that you and your man are better suited than he and the Sagittarius were.

Cancer

According to everything you know about relationships, a man needs to be cared for, and a comfortable home needs to be established and maintained. The wayward, fun-loving Sagittarius didn't see things that way. She usually leaves men feeling... nervous. He never knew how long they'd last, so he put little actual stock in the long term when he was with her. With you, he will know that he is loved and needed, and that there will always be a home for him to return to after a hard day at work. As for the Sag, she's moved on, and that makes things between the two of you much easier. She'll be nice and cordial, and at worst she will ignore you. Be aware that any overtures of friendship she makes toward you might not be genuine, and that anything she does that hurts you isn't necessarily directed at you or done because she doesn't like you. You've just gotten in her way.

Leo

There isn't much for you to do about the Sagittarius ex. Due to your fire-sign affinity, the two of you together can easily ignite an inferno. Your interactions are hysterical, if the two of you get along, and if not...everyone needs to stand back. You should remember that both of you are very protective, and much of the conflict between you is due to your desire to protect the ones you love. You aren't afraid of her, because you are confident that your new relationship can withstand whatever she throws at it, and she isn't afraid of you either. She won't take your boisterous personality as a threat, and you will be calmed by her humanitarian personality. Because she was never very good at commitment, the devotion you give to your man is as welcome as a warm fire on a cold night. When you love a man, he knows it.

Virgo

Your man's relationship with the Sagittarius left a lot to be desired. If there is one thing that you readily give your companions, it is devotion. You cannot understand how anyone could be in a relationship and not be true to their lover. After all, what is the point of being in a relationship anyway? The horror stories your man could tell you about all his sleepless nights, worried sick that she was with another man and never getting the gratification of an explanation from her, will make you want to cry. How could the poor man put up with that for so long? The Sagittarius will try to use friendship to disable your new relationship with her ex, but you'll be able to see through her tactics. That doesn't mean that you won't try to be her friend, because you probably will (she's just too nice and tactful not to be friends with), but you will never let her get close to her ex again. And, with the Sag, that's what will make a difference.

Libra

The largest problem that a Libran has with a Sagittarius is usually a small annoyance about the Sag's escapist and playful personality. The chance of the two of you having any major blowup is small, as both of you tend to avoid conflict and prefer to stay on the good side of people. As a Libran, you are skilled in the art of relationships and romance, commitment and love. The Sag was more lackadaisical in her approach, and had a lot of trouble being committed to her partner. Your man is probably already finding out that dating a Libran woman is similar to being in a classic romantic film—the actors are glamorous and witty, the stage is classy, and the script is grandiose.

Scorpio

While most fire and water signs have difficulty getting along even in the best of times, the two of you have empathy for one another. Despite being practical jokers, the Sag is one of the most mature signs in the zodiac, and she is usually very calm when facing a conflict. You can appreciate her distance from your new relationship, and unlike with other signs, the Sagittarius isn't likely to use the guise of friendship as a way of getting her ex back when he is with you. After all, you are a Scorpio and you can see through most manipulation, and you view most attempts to manipulate you as a personal insult to your intelligence that will not be tolerated. You will be a more committed and intense partner than the emotionally aloof Sagittarius. While the Centaur is wise, your intelligence is piercing and can startle those around you (and sometimes, even yourself). Any relationship you have will be extreme and adventurous, full of witty, philosophical discussions that many men find exciting.

Sagittarius

As with all same-sign conflicts, you know how to anticipate the attacks (if any) that will come from the Sagittarius, because you are aware of her strengths and weaknesses. The biggest conflict that arises between you is that you are so much alike. She doesn't understand why her ex picked you over her, and you don't understand exactly how to save your relationship from ending like theirs did. You will need to find solace in your individuality, and realize that there are many differences between you. When you do stumble across similarities between your new relationship and his old one, laugh about them and move on. It's only a big deal if you make it into one.

Capricorn

There isn't much that the two of you agree on, but both of you are capable of avoiding any outright conflict. As an ex, the Sag doesn't stick around for long, and once she's gone, she'll be gone for good, leaving you and your man to form a new life together. The life your man is beginning with you will be full of successes and triumphs, plans and possessions. You will make sure that he reaches his full potential, and that he knows he has you to thank for it. The Sagittarius wasn't big on commitment, and you aren't one to casually commit to a long shot, so your man had better be prepared for a lasting relationship with you.

Aquarius

You and the Sagittarius have a good chance of getting along, because both of you understand the importance of respect and are willing to give it, even in a situation like this. You have a silliness about you that the Sag finds entertaining, and her quick mind and rational beliefs complement your own. If anything negative happens between you, it will be a fluke born on the wings of chance rather than potential, and should be treated like an accident, because the Sag probably didn't mean anything by it. As a lover, you are more committed to your partner than the Sagittarius was, and you are more concerned about the long-term potential of the affair. Anything you do will be for the benefit of yourself and your relationship, not just because you had a whim to do something.

Pisces

By nature, the Sagittarius is both a wizened human and a beast (after all, the representation of Sag is a Centaur—both human and horse), and the fact that you can never quite pin one down leaves you feeling a little unstable. That fact that no one can pin you down either doesn't really matter, because most of the time you have little problem understanding yourself. Anyway, you and the Centaur were never meant to be friends in the casual sense. There is a definite tension in all of your interactions, and you can't help but think that the Sagittarius is more than willing to make jokes at your expense. In a very real way, you are more mature than the Sag (even though she is one of the most mature signs in the zodiac), and it is much easier for most men to relate to mature women rather than a Sagittarius, who is often either a raucous clown or a lording philosopher.

Capricorn

The *Capricorn* Ex-Girlfriend

Dates: December 22–January 20
Planet: Saturn
Element: Cardinal earth
Representation: Goat, often depicted with the tail of a fish

Any man who has come into contact with a female Capricorn will most likely have two extra holes in his rear end from her charging at him so many times. She is one woman who isn't famous for having soft, compliant ways. She knows what she wants from life, and is willing to do whatever is necessary to get it. The Capricorn woman is the most likely of all the signs to be a gold digger. She is most concerned about her financial status and social position, and doesn't care if she truly loves the man she is with, although she would prefer it if she did. Your man, the poor little guy, was likely just a rung on the ladder—a means to gain a higher position who obviously wasn't quite high enough to keep her interest.

Cold, calculating, frigid, and snobbish, this woman is the ideal companion for any banker or businessman who is only looking for a wife to increase his stature, or who is emotionally vacant. A few of the poor souls who wind up in bed with a Goat long for an emotionally available companion, one who actually cares about them rather than their bank account and connections, but their decision to continue the relationship proves that they are gluttons for punishment. If you have gotten one of these few, count yourself lucky and give him a hug—he needs it. If you have the first type of man, be careful of his intentions.

The Goat surrounds herself with minions who are lesser than she—people who can make her feel superior and needed. It is now your job to watch out for this clique, as rumors will abound about you and your man. Social position is so important to this woman that any ending of a love affair must be quickly followed up by social alliance. Needless to say, she probably took a great deal of her ex's friends with her when she went. And oh yes, it was she who left him, no matter who did the actual walking. She is rational and bitter about their ending, but not so much so as to raise rumors about herself. It isn't that the Goat is completely emotionally vacant; she's just learned that love can hurt, so she's careful about how she shows it. She also has fears, hopes, and disappointments, but those too are quickly ignored because of their overwhelming immensity.

Does she want him back? No, but she would like him to want to come back. Now that he's with you (and make sure he is *openly* with you), that doesn't seem too likely. This assault to her dignity must be countered. It will be countered. She will pass him off as a casual affair, and if they were married, she will claim that some personal deficiency on his part led him to divorce her, or her to divorce him. Perhaps he was looking for too much attention, or maybe he was too demanding or even too experimental in bed. Maybe he challenged her too much, or questioned her too thoroughly about her whereabouts or child-rearing practices. This is one woman who must have the final say in all decisions, and she expects complacent submission.

She is stubborn and resourceful in her decision making, rarely allowing her emotions to lead her, although her moods play a large part in what she does. In fact, even though her moods are behind nearly every action, she will be able to come up with a logical explanation that removes all blame from herself. She is never wrong—everybody else is. And if they'd only listen to her more, they would see a definite improvement in their lives. Unfortunately, it's not as if this feeling of hers lacks any evidence. She *is* successful, and she *has* earned some honest respect, and people *have* benefited from her advice. However, her constant self-righteousness left your man feeling useless and awkward. He was made to second-guess not only every move he made, but the reasons behind anything he did.

I know of one poor man who was reduced to a stuttering pansy whenever his overbearing Capricorn wife entered the room. So, it should come as no surprise if your man is incapable of standing up for himself when dealing with her as an ex. He's been so beaten down for such a long time that there just isn't anything left to fight with. Boost his ego a little bit and help him develop some backbone, and hopefully he'll improve.

If There Are Children Involved

If she pays any attention to them, it will be to discipline and control them. She has a knack for making her offspring feel incompetent and upset. However, she most likely will not be much of a presence in their lives. She is self-centered and too concerned with her own position to care much about theirs—other than how their actions affect her.

What He Misses

Well...um...her stability? The Capricorn knew how to provide a structured home, where everything had its place and things were taken care of without her man having to lift a finger. If he enjoys his social position as much as she did, then he might miss her influence and reassurance. He might also miss having a significant other who doesn't mind being a part of an emotionally reserved relationship—someone who is concerned only with how influential and important he is instead of how loving and caring.

What He Doesn't Miss

Her moods. And all of the reasons she gave to justify her moods and how they affected her life. He won't miss being used for his social position or his bank account. He won't miss the lack of physical attention and companionship. He won't miss being flaunted to her loser friends, being a pawn on her chessboard and demeaned in her bed. She demands accountability from everyone around her and yet denies that she is responsible for anything.

What You Can Do to Piss Her Off

Have more friends, more money, and more fun than she does. Or, be more moral and philosophical—beating down her own beliefs and showing that you are much better than she is. Be an equal to your man, or even more successful than he is, and enjoy it. Either renounce her values as vain, or beat her at her own social game. A man once asked his Capricorn ex-girlfriend what he had to do to win her back, and she replied, "Become the most powerful man in the world, and then I will come back." Finally faced with the truth of her pride, he answered, "If I was the most powerful man in the world, then why would I settle for *you*?" For the first time in her life, someone questioned her value. She was so startled that she couldn't find a response. If her worth wasn't obvious, then why defend herself to the ignorant? But, somewhere deep inside, she wondered if he was right.

How Your Sign Will Handle the Situation

Aries

The issues between you and the Capricorn ex have a deeper root than just the situation the two of you find yourselves in at the moment. She is envious of your passion and ingenuousness, and the way that some people find your naiveté to be charming is maddening to her. She will never have your air of seductive voluptuousness, and your man is grateful that his new love is more than capable in the bedroom... and everywhere else. You are a great date, and many a head has turned when you walked by. On some level, she was a bit more down-to-earth and stable than you are, but I'm sure your new man won't mind trading in a mortgage for two airline tickets to the Bahamas.

Taurus

Both you and the Capricorn speak the same language, and you understand each other's nonverbal cues as well. But this situation could very easily turn into a "hold your enemies close" type of thing. Even though the both of you are very earthy creatures, most of the negativity between the two of you is based in the ethereal realm of thoughts and psychoses rather than physical or verbal actualities. The way you think about the situation and the Capricorn will greatly affect the way you handle things. It's best if you concentrate on building your new relationship on a strong two-person foundation and leave the exes in the past, far behind you. You are more seductive and tranquil than the Capricorn is, and your man is sure to find many qualities in you that surpass those of the Goat. Yes, the Goat may be a cardinal sign, but you have Venus (your ruler) on your side.

Gemini

There's no one better than a Gemini to disrupt the doldrums of "normal" life. You seek adventure and are constantly on the lookout for something rare and meaningful. Every man you meet hopes that he will be the answer to your lonely heart. The Capricorn lacks the seeking quality you have, the desperate search for meaning, which makes her seem one-dimensional and boring in comparison to you. Your taste for adventure adds excitement to your relationships, and your ability to reason and discuss makes you an intriguing partner. How do I know he's in love with you? It's easy. You're a Gemini, and Geminis are the charmers of the zodiac.

Cancer

Even though both of you are cardinal signs, the two of you have been in direct opposition to each other from birth. There will always be tension between you, and the situation the two of you face now will not help anything. As the new girlfriend, you feel that your position (at least in the beginning) isn't as strong as you'd like it to be, and when you are going up against the mountainous Goat, you are afraid that your new relationship might suffer. The Goat is demanding, and you are at first compliant and easily pushed around. Soon, though, your cardinal aspect will come into play, and you will start to rebel against the Capricorn's falsely assumed authority. The Goat will balk, but will have to come to terms with your new position in her ex's life. As a girlfriend, you can provide more emotional support than the Goat can, and you make your man feel that he has more to offer than a bulging bank account and a blue-blood family name.

Leo

The warmth that radiates from the sunny Lioness can melt even the coldest of hearts. You are a joyful lover who revels in sex and attention. Your man isn't used to it, and for the first couple of months with you he's likely to be exhausted...in a good way. The confining attitude of the Capricorn is often accompanied by an air of judgment. The combination makes you feel unwelcome and diminished, and it probably made your man feel the same way. It is through her "authority" that she attempts to control you, and she will try to remove any power you have over her ex. She isn't happy with the trade he's made, and she openly doesn't think much of you. Even if the two of you get along, you can't help but feel that she is never laughing *with* you but is instead laughing *at* you. It is time to reclaim your old confidence and stand up to the Goat. *You* are a lioness. *You* are at the top of the food chain. Goats *flee* from you. Remember?

Virgo

Because both of you can rise above the situation that has brought you together, there is a good chance that there will be real affection and respect between you...as long as she never criticizes your man. You are very devoted to your partners, and even though you can point out their many imperfections, you don't appreciate it when anyone else does. Especially one of their exes. You are rational, and you understand that some things went wrong in their relationship, so you don't expect them to be on the best terms now that their relationship has failed. But the ex needs to recognize your position, and that you hope that everything will work out in your new relationship. With a little conversation, and a little wheedling, the Capricorn should be able to come to that understanding.

Libra

Whenever a Libra and a Capricorn meet in anger, the argument quickly becomes about which one is the most shallow, and then it moves on to whose morals are the most ethical, and whose integrity is the most bombproof. While the two of you can usually get along under normal circumstances, the present conflict you find yourselves in could keep you from becoming true friends. However, both of you will try to make the best of the situation. Your man is now with a true romantic, and if he's the one to make you bloom, he's a lucky man and knows it. She might have provided a good home, but you will help your love build a good *relationship*. After all, Libra is the sign of marriage.

Scorpio

The Capricorn woman is more respectful of your presence than she is with most other signs. Both you and she have strived to achieve something with your lives, and you both want authority and power in your business pursuits. Because you have similar goals, you find it easy to empathize with each other. The fact that the Goat is somewhat more stable than you are may make you a little fearful about the permanence of your new relationship. However, you must remember that their relationship ended for a reason. Obviously, things were not nearly as perfect as the Capricorn would like you to think they were. You can bring more emotions and passion to a relationship than she could, and you are more protective and supportive. You know that fear you have of not being good enough? Well, don't forget to let it go every now and then, okay?

Sagittarius

What you value in life is very different from what the Capricorn does. For example, she is a materialistic person, and while you understand that some of your adventures require financing, the value of *acquiring* money just for the sake of keeping it is completely foreign to you. She also craves social standing and has to fight for it, whereas you tend to stumble upon it accidentally, mostly due to your outgoing personality. The Capricorn may flit about for a little while, waiting to see if her ex is going to come running back, but once she understands that he is gone for good, she will go and find herself a new companion. Any rumors she leaves in her wake won't bother you either. You are used to rumors following you—it's one of the prices you pay for your adventures and your independence.

Capricorn

Because the Capricorn is an idealist, and it's rare for two people to have the same concept of an ideal, the two of you may in fact be more different from each other than most other same-sign combinations are. However, there are enough similarities between you to form a friendship, if both of you want one. You understand where she is coming from, and you know that eventually she will completely let go of her ex and find someone more suited to her plans of success. You, too, are able to find eager replacements for the men you have left behind. That doesn't mean you didn't love them. In a way, you still do and always will, but you accept that they are a part of your past, not your future.

Aquarius

The Capricorn woman is only interested in money and status. While she does have a philosophical and intelligent mind, she rarely uses it to penetrate the deeper mysteries that you are interested in.

Her mundane mindset is completely uninteresting, and you are unsympathetic to her insecurities. After all, you are the new girlfriend, so exactly why should you feel any sympathy for her? You understand where she's coming from, but it doesn't go much further beyond that. You will provide an intellectual companionship for your new man, supporting him in the furtherance of his mind and soul. With her, he had only physical security; with you, everything else is taken care of as well.

Pisces

You feel a strange sense of comfort with the Capricorn, even if she is your lover's ex. She is steady and stable, and you can't help but feel protected by her. This is one of the astrological partnerships that can result in friendship despite the situation the two of you are in, making your life much easier than it could have been. Unless the ending of the Capricorn's relationship with your man was ugly, he will probably appreciate that the two of you can get along so well. The only thing you need to watch out for is making sure that your allegiance belongs first to your man and then to his ex, and not the other way around. You are more compassionate than the Capricorn was, and you are not nearly so tied to material possessions. Strengthen your commitment to your new relationship, and make sure that both of you are getting your needs met.

Aquarius

The *Aquarius* Ex-Girlfriend

Dates: January 21–February 19
Planet: Uranus
Element: Fixed air
Representation: Water Bearer

The *water bearer*? She's an *air* sign with "aqua" in her name, and her representation is a water bearer? Confusing. What is a water bearer anyway? It's a vessel. An urn. A hurricane. In essence, she claims to be made up of things that are in fact no part in her but are instead temporary pieces of luggage. Contradiction and a faulty sense of personal power and accomplishment follow this woman around like the smell of cheap perfume. She thinks very highly of herself, and not many of the reasons behind such an inflated ego are rational or concrete. She is important because she is important. And don't mess with her, or else. Out of the many aggressive signs in the zodiac, Aquarius is the best known for having restraining orders issued against her.

Every Aquarius is invariably drawn to religion, and they are not happy until they are an authority of that religion. This means that they tend to fill themselves up with everybody else's opinions and ideals, and then spew forth rehearsed dogma and claim themselves to be learned women. They do little to verify their beliefs, but they can justify them until they are blue in the face. Unable to beat an opponent on their own, they seek some sort of authority to back them up. Their wars are malicious and silly, with little actual accomplishment. As with all other air signs, gossip and rumors are a constant threat. The Aquarius is so cowardly that she will not do any harm for which she could be blamed if it fails. However, if her tactics succeed she will do all she can to claim the credit.

If your man spent much time with his Aquarius, he probably experienced a lot of personal freedom, not realizing that she was watching him every time he went out. She set up spies at every social function who reported back to her about his movements. The sense of freedom was a false feeling, something he might have discovered upon the ending of their tryst. The breakup did not go particularly smoothly because this woman's ego is so wrapped up in everything she does. And, as a form of vengeance, she will seek to hurt his ego and reputation as well as yours. Even quiet Aquarians are defensive of their pride, so don't let shyness fool you. Any Aquarius can hold a grudge for years, sometimes coming back a decade later to harangue an ex for things that he did way back when. Does this mean that she'll be a part of your life for years? Probably.

Often, the Aquarius woman only feigned attraction and love. She is typically so withdrawn from the rest of humanity—and a function of her ego is to support and explain this loneliness—that actual emotion is never anything more than a stage on which she acts out the drama of her oh-so-powerful life. Their relationship was full of power plays rather than passionate emotions. He was often an opponent to her, rather than a companion, especially if he started expressing his own ideas and beliefs. If he was content to walk ten paces behind her, and not look her in the eye when they conversed, then he probably is a lot more messed up than you want to deal with.

On the other hand, the Aquarius woman is so impressionable when meeting someone of authority that she can be easily led to adopt another's personality and lifestyle. Because of this trait, she often flits from one belief system to another, following the trends of power and influence. There is a certain vulnerability to an Aquarius that often inspires men to be protective of her. The passion the Aquarian has for religion and humanity pushes her to help others who are less fortunate. Even if she was a fickle follower, she followed with all her heart.

If There Are Children Involved

The Aquarian mother is more a friend to her children, wanting them to love and respect her. She is somewhat detached and unable to show real devotion because her heart always belongs to her ego or to a belief. She likes to think that she is a knowledgeable teacher, and will spend much time teaching her children about religion and philosophy. She will not appreciate it if you are of a different religion than she is and attempt to have the children participate in it.

What He Misses

The apparent freedom that she awarded him. The sense of being around someone knowledgeable and powerful. The intellectual conversations, the religious devotion, and the support of his career. She is a woman who lives in her head, and as such she could be a detached lover and friend. She was jealous and possessive, despite giving him the feeling of being free, and he mistook that for being loved and desired.

What He Doesn't Miss

Her sudden and irrational anger. Her insistence that vengeance is to be expected for any wrong he committed. Her belief that her own ego was reality, and that instead of being a silly fake, she was a powerful woman. Her ego also led her to be paranoid—fearing that everyone who tried to dismantle her ego was actually trying to take away her power. Her absolute blind faith in the words of others, and her inability to come up with new ideas on her own, was tiring and annoying to watch. She simply cannot perceive the world without her in it.

What You Can Do to Piss Her Off

Constantly call her bluff. Every time she espouses some ridiculous belief, argue it with her and prove her wrong. Or, you can just ignore her and gain power and esteem for yourself. The best idea is to create a world without her in it, one in which you do not seek to appease her or argue against her. Fighting with her keeps your attention on her, and gives her unwarranted status and regard. It's also a good idea that your man doesn't see you in a power struggle with her, as that type of war was something he had hoped to leave behind.

How Your Sign Will Handle the Situation

Aries

The Aquarian woman takes one cool look at your liveliness and quickly decides that you are too open and chatty to be wise, logical, or respectable. You take a look at her complacent dedication to the latest trends and decide she's a superficial pseudo-intellectual. Your judgment is closer to the truth than hers is. Luckily, your man is almost guaranteed to have a better time with you than with the aloof Aquarius. And, he'll quickly see the sensitive, caring, intelligent woman that lies beneath your façade of being a fun-loving socialite. The Aquarian can do little besides blow hot air.

Taurus

It is completely beyond you how *that woman* can get away with so many egotistical ramblings when she obviously has very little to back them up. Here's a clue: Anyone who is around her for any length of time has simply gotten used to it. Watch their eyes when she begins to profess her strengths... they're rolling. If you are still doubtful, ask your man how he put up with her boasts for so long. He ignored her most of the time, that's how. After a week or two of being around the Water Bearer, it's rare that anyone believes a word she says, and most people stop listening to her at all. Your steady personality and your humbleness further your social standing and increase the respect people have for you. Your new lover is just one of many who appreciate your honesty and trustworthiness.

Gemini

Both you and the Aquarian woman have a need for freedom in your relationships. The difference is that you enjoy freedom to pursue your own interests, and if a lover happens to leave while you are away on an adventure, you will feel upset for a while and then quickly find yourself a new playmate. The Aquarius, however, is different. She expects her lovers to dutifully await her return. And if they don't, her hidden possessiveness takes hold and her ego becomes tangled in the situation, making her a nasty ex-girlfriend even if it is her fault that the relationship ended. Her tantrums and rumor-spreading will begin to take a toll on your new relationship, so it's best if your man severs ties with the Aquarius completely. You're a lot more fun than the Aquarius was, and you lack her self-centeredness. Your man stands to be much happier with you than he was with her, and he will be happier still if the influence she had in his life dies alongside their relationship.

Cancer

Although you typically remain inside of your protective shell whenever you are confronted by a fierce opponent, there is something about the Aquarian's ego that won't let you back down from a fight with her. You will be nice and tactful, but your claws are always ready. You simply aren't afraid of the Water Bearer, and you are one of the few signs that isn't. The first thing you learned as a little girl was how to be safe and comfortable in your home life, and because you have been building defenses around your private domain for years, there is little that the Aquarius can do to harm you. If your man has proven himself worthy and reliable, then he is more than welcome inside your secure abode, and the both of you can weather the Aquarian storm together in comfort.

Leo

The Aquarian is very arrogant and lacks the self-deprecating humor that you have about your own pride, which makes her almost impossible to deal with because you are always having to walk on eggshells to avoid bruising her fragile ego. Actually, instead of walking on eggshells, as a Lion you would much rather find a way to trip her up and then eat her. But you'd do better playing defense and making sure that your new relationship is safe, because the Aquarius is known for her vindictive and spiteful schemes, and logic or ethics rarely stop her from trying to hurt someone. Just keep in mind the many positive attributes you bring to your new relationship. You are passionate and protective, fun to hang around, and always full of excitement and drama. Your interests may not match those of the Water Bearer, but that is hardly a downfall. You are your own person, and you are wildly unique—there should be no reason for a Lion to fear an Aquarius.

Virgo

Although in other circumstances the two of you would have much to teach one another, and you both would profit from a friendship, the chance that the two of you will develop even an acquaintanceship is small. The differences between you are too great, and both you and the Water Bearer have a tendency to be overly critical of others. Any argument between you is never fully dealt with because both of you will quickly blow it out of proportion. For example, if she says that you are too clingy as a girlfriend, then the conflict quickly turns into whether or not she's trying to say she was a better girlfriend than you are. Aside from any conflict you have with her, the new relationship with your love has a chance of being a good one—if you are careful not to obsess over his past. You have so much to give as a girlfriend, and you are a devoted lover, so focus your attention on him—he'll be thankful for it.

Libra

The fact that many of the Aquarian's beliefs and opinions are spouted with the obsessive dedication of a bad PR campaign annoys you. You can respect a person for having the strength to uphold unpopular beliefs, but her lack of balance, good judgment, originality, and authenticity makes you question if she actually deserves respect. It is not hard to see that she goes where the power is, never realizing that it is not her own and instead cloaking herself in someone else's authority. You, a lover of justice and a born judge, see through her act, and she dislikes the exposure. In general, you are similar to your fellow air sign in your intelligence and fickleness, but you have a realism and an open mindset that she will never have. For once, your man is with someone he can really be proud of, and not someone who demands respect she doesn't deserve. Unfortunately, the lack of respect that you have for the Aquarius will infuriate her and possibly help her rationalize the need to get back at you—to "demand" your respect. The situation is probably not a pleasant one, and there is little chance of a friendship between you, so it would be best to ignore her entirely (especially because you *hate* confrontation and conflict).

Scorpio

You are a deeply loving woman who is involved in your lover's life and interested in who he really is and what he really thinks. You see through people easily, and you simply don't tolerate any falsehoods. The Aquarius is interested in who people really are too, but she doesn't have your stinging intelligence to help her see through other people's masks. Both of you are suspicious, and this suspicion is now turned against each other. To be honest, when I think of the two of you in a conflict, I flinch. Both of you can be malicious, and the Aquarian's hurt ego means that she probably won't pull punches when she's dealing with you. And because you are in a position in which you need to protect yourself and your lover, you're not likely to hold anything back either. Both of you should rationally agree not to like each other, and move on. The Aquarius deserves better than to be focused on her past, and you have a wonderful new life to build with your man.

Sagittarius

Unlike many other signs, you don't have any problems with the Aquarius—unless she has done something specifically against you. You are a master of walking on eggshells, and you know how to maneuver your way around fragile egos without disturbing them. You also know how to separate your new relationship from their old one, and you accept that people can change, so you don't expect your man to act in your relationship like he used to in theirs. With you, he is getting a new beginning, and you will let the Aquarius know that if she is to be a presence in your life, she will have to play by your rules. Respect is key, and you can get it from the Water Bearer more easily than she usually gives it. You are just as intelligent as she is, and you have an empathy for humanity and a passion for your lovers that can make you an ideal companion—be it a love interest for your man or a friend for his ex.

Capricorn

When it comes to social status, you and the Aquarius are on similar pages. Both of you yearn for a position of respect among your peers, and because of this shared interest, the two of you know how best to hurt one another. Yes, your time would be better spent on other things, but the Aquarius might not let you and your man walk away unscathed. Protect yourself, and don't let the Water Bearer in on any problems that you and your man might be having, as she might use that as a weapon against you as well. There is always the need to be careful of where one is stepping when one crosses a Water Bearer, but who is better at finding a path through the danger than an earthy Goat?

Aquarius

Two Aquarians put together can make a very odd pair. Any argument between you will be fought out on the ethereal plane of egos and assumptions. Because the two of you have the same sun sign, you know what her main weaknesses are and how to push her buttons in the most effective manner. However, you are less likely to be attacked by this woman than by, say, a Scorpio. Because of your similarities, the Water Bearer is less suspicious of you than she is of most others, because you understand each other's motivations and behavior. You have no problem remembering that even though you and your man's ex are alike in many ways, you are a unique individual who can bring a lot to the relationship that she couldn't. You can see how she acted in their old relationship, and you can avoid her mistakes. You are a charming woman, full of wit and intuition, insight and eccentricities. Dating you is never boring.

Pisces

As a sign that is well versed in the truth beyond all widely held beliefs and dreams, you have difficulty understanding how the Aquarian claims to know everything. In all honesty, the Aquarian would benefit from having long discussions with you on current trends in philosophy and religion, because you would be able to point out how so many of her views are a product of her environment and not exactly of truth. Your man is likely to notice that you are wise and humble, whereas the Aquarian was loud and boastful. He will benefit from discussions with you. All you have to do is be willing to open up about your thoughts.

Pisces

The *Pisces* Ex-Girlfriend

Dates: February 20–March 20
Planet: Neptune
Element: Mutable water
Representation: Two Fish chasing each other's tails

Not only are Piscean women the most delusional of any sign in the zodiac, but they are also compulsive liars and manipulators. And, dating a Pisces woman is about as much fun as being trapped on the wrong side of the looking glass for the rest of your life. Everything that can be backwards, is. Everywhere you turn, bizarre new objects, people, and situations come into light—ultimately leaving you with a feeling of *Oh my God, what have I done?* And then comes the best part—a giant monster waiting to eat you, a jabberwocky of gigantic proportions. Every Pisces woman has one, if not twenty, of these creatures lurking in her self-created world.

Almost immediately upon being ushered into the world of the Piscean female, most people begin to search desperately for an exit. Some rely on the truths of "reality" to lead them from such nonsense, but "reality" has little bearing on a Piscean. In fact, she will do all she can to avoid reality, because reality destroys her magic. Instead, she lives in a self-created universe with herself at the center and everyone else floating around her, held to her by the Piscean's amazing gravitational pull. This doesn't mean that she is a physically large woman; it's more that her personality and feigned need for protection force others into a set role. I'm not trying to say that the world of the Pisces is bad. In fact, many people enjoy her ethereal imaginings. And her intense dislike of truth can help a man feel like anything is possible.

The Pisces is always looking for people to protect her, perhaps due to the ever-present monsters in her world. Any mistakes she makes are quickly blamed on someone else, and she projects her image of being a victim far and wide. Because of this projection, and because of her assumed persona of being a powerless and compassionate woman, she mostly attracts men who feel an overwhelming need to protect someone, and who don't mind getting little in return for their efforts. This need makes them easy targets for her, as they are also the type of men that most readily accept blame and fall for guilt trips—her two favorite games. After all, how do you argue with someone who refuses to be logical and unemotional? You can't. You just can't. You either leave, or give in—sacrificing a part of yourself in order to accommodate her. This aforementioned type of man usually does the latter, making him more of a fixer-upper than a ready-made man.

In many astrological works, the Pisces is often heralded as the most compassionate sign in the zodiac. However, unless there will be a film crew or some other form of audience, the Pisces will not be involved in the project. In all honesty and bitterness, the only reason that Pisceans are compassionate is to further their own interests and to help promote their image of being a martyr. They never do anything for someone else unless it will bring recognition and honor to themselves. Because of this, they often exploit the real victims, without bringing actual benefit to the situation. This attitude was reflected in the Piscean's relationship with your man, whom she never did anything for unless she was highly praised for it. Many Pisceans even refuse to work for a living, and instead depend on the men they are with, or their parents, to support them. This habit is just another extension of their inability to be held accountable for their actions.

The Piscean woman is also a wayward lover, who often refuses to give more during sex than she can get. She could be cold and distant during their lovemaking, inciting feelings of guilt and desperation in her lover. Imagine how *you'd* feel if every week or month you were having sex with a clammy salmon (figuratively, of course), wondering if the flailing fish was enjoying your technique or just flopping around in hopes of finding a fishbowl somewhere.

Despite her lack of enthusiasm in bed, do not be surprised if your new beau still harbors a need to protect and appease this woman, perhaps even going so far as cheating when she shows an inclination to start their love affair once more. Many men who deal with a Pisces woman never get a sense of closure, as she is always attempting to keep men at her beck and call. If possible, she will never fully end the relationship, but instead leave the breakup questionable so that she may come back if she so desires. She keeps a list of possible relationships, and she is seldom single because she needs so much attention.

My advice to you is to leave her far behind and make sure your man's fishing days are over.

If There Are Children Involved

She will do all she can to make them adore her. However, her attention is sporadic, as children have an evolutionary tendency to be quite self-centered themselves, which conflicts with her own selfishness. The children will quickly learn to either care for themselves, or care for her—feeling the need to protect their victim mother from the world at large. She will distrust your position in their lives, and could quite possibly use the children against you. Try to make sure that they are independent individuals, stress their personal accountability, and never say anything against their mother. But try not to lie.

What He Misses

Her need for protection made him feel wanted and necessary. It gave his life a purpose that it was probably lacking before they got together. Her otherworldliness gave their romance a sense of the magical. Her quietude led him to falsely believe that everything was fine.

What He Doesn't Miss

Her emotional pleas and the need to appease and assure her constantly. Her need for reassurance often stemmed from her own lack of commitment, a lesson he discovered too late. The guilt trips and blame games that were assigned to him left him feeling vacant and inadequate. Her refusal to face reality was an escapist tactic and put pressure on him to handle their problems.

What You Can Do to Piss Her Off

Live your life in reality and don't play by her rules. Just because she rejects logic doesn't mean that you or your man should. Under the best circumstances, you will be able to ignore her. However, your man was her caretaker and will probably have a difficult time abandoning his duties. Remind him that she is a grown woman who is more than capable of taking care of herself, and then push him away from the fishing pole. Rotting fish smell, so she will most likely make a bigger and bigger stink about their separation as time goes on in an attempt to make your life hell. Do your best to ignore her.

How Your Sign Will Handle the Situation

Aries

Your direct approach to life and blatant self-assurance will throw the mutable Pisces into a tailspin. Conversely, her avoidance of reality and manipulative nature will infuriate you. If things get tough, you will want to confront her, just to get it out of the way, but she will slip through your grasp at every turn. Before you know it, you are the bad guy and the end of her relationship was your fault, as well as everything else that has gone wrong in her life since then. Your new guy will love your straightforward attitude and be grateful that he's now with a woman who knows who she is. Your passion and idealism are enough to keep any man enthralled. The Pisces has nothing on you, babe.

Taurus

You are grounded and earthy, whereas she is spacey and an escapist. You can't understand how she comes to the conclusions she does, and her inability to take control of her life leaves little room for friendship or understanding between the two of you.

However, arguments will tend to spin out of control because you simply have no tolerance for people like her, and she will do little besides claim you are the aggressor and demand that her ex protect her. Your man will be thankful for your concern about him and his welfare, and your ability to make his home comfortable and secure. Unless he has a hatred for reality or a need to have a fantasy life alongside his actual one, he is much more stable with you than her.

Gemini

There isn't much about the Pisces that you can understand. She isn't logical, so rationally discussing the situation the two of you find yourselves in isn't going to work. She is constantly passive-aggressive, so you can't discuss the basis of a problem or its resolution with her without getting frustrated. You need to understand that she is a Fish, and as such she is slippery and squeamish, and apt to turn tail and flit away the moment she feels a ripple in the water. Your new relationship will be more of a partnership than his relationship with her was, and you are a lot more fun to be around. Make sure that you don't become too pessimistic and sarcastic with her or with your love.

Cancer

You can sympathize with the Pisces' position. You know what it feels like to have the rug pulled out from under you, even if you did deserve it. The two of you won't enter into a real argument because she can sense your empathy for her, and the Pisces would rather have you (and everyone else in the world) as a friend than as an enemy. Even so, your new man will feel a sense of security with you that he never felt with the Pisces. You will build a home that you live in *together*, while the Pisces had a home both in actuality and in a world of fantasy. You may retreat into a shell when you are hurt, but the Pisces can spend months or years at the bottom of the ocean for no better reason than liking the temperature better there.

Leo

If any sign in the zodiac could be guaranteed that they won't have any problem with a Pisces woman, it would be the Leo. Your demanding sense of competency and control gives the Pisces little room in which to negotiate or manipulate. You might find yourself becoming her protector, because every Pisces has a deep desire to be controlled (to have someone else take accountability for her life), and you love to control. If, during a conflict, she brands herself as the victim, you are much more likely to agree with her than the other signs are, and you will quickly follow the pronouncement with a litany of all the ways that she is weaker than you. As for your man, he's now with a woman who is all woman (and a little cat), and although your sense of possibility is as great as the Piscean's, you often have a plan to achieve your ends.

Virgo

While picking through a box of old things the Pisces left behind (the Pisces manages to leave some of her things *everywhere* she's ever been), you can quickly come up with a list of reasons that your life is much better than hers. You are organized and stable, and you base your life in reality. You are aware that there is negativity in the world, and that it isn't your fault or directed only at you. You can also understand why your man is so confused at the moment. After being underwater with a Pisces for so long, a man is bound to feel a little out of sorts on land, not to mention a bit pruny. It's obvious to you that he is much better off now that he's away from her, and he probably agrees.

Libra

At first you can't believe the stories your new man tells you about what it was like living with the Pisces. What does he mean everything was filthy, no furniture matched, she hardly worked, and he couldn't have a decent conversation with her? How could he stand it? Well, he's definitely getting something different with you. You know how to take care of your man without losing yourself in the process, and you can be a charming partner and hostess. Instead of the constant negativity he dealt with in his old relationship, you are supportive and caring and help to build his self-esteem. There's a good chance he's not missing her at all.

Scorpio

Surprisingly, your jealousy will not be immediately triggered by the Pisces ex. At first you feel a desire to protect this wayward creature from the harshness of life, and she will encourage you to act in such a way. It's not until after you discover that her weakness is a form of manipulation that you start to react poorly to her presence. You begin to see how so much of what she does and says is manipulative, and as any strong woman would feel, you don't appreciate being used. Neither did your man, and that's why he's no longer with her. You are more responsible, caring, passionate, and real than the Pisces could ever hope to be. You are honestly *there* for your man, and I'm sure he's grateful for it.

Sagittarius

Adventurous and fun-loving, you can't stand the thought of retreating into deep water every time something new and interesting comes your way. Your wise personality feels deeply unsettled—almost *seasick*—at the thought of being as wishy-washy as the Pisces is about life. You have so many things to do in so little time, and you love the thought of taking your new man along for the ride (or better yet, maybe he has his own adventures in mind). Your new relationship is sure to be a thrilling one, and will be nothing like his old relationship was. This can be either too much of a good thing or just the right amount of fun, depending on the sign of your lover. But I'm sure that in either scenario, your sense of humor will help ease his transition from boring to electrifying.

Capricorn

Surprisingly, you have an innate ability to understand and comfort the dethroned Piscean woman. Your stable presence is reassuring to her, and she will probably be glad that if anyone had to take over her role in her ex's life that it would be you, a woman whom she believes will at least keep a place open in his life for an ex-girlfriend to become a friend. How far you actually want to take this is up to you, and you can pretty much expect the Piscean to submit to any boundary you draw. Submit? Yes, eventually, as long as you give her constant reminders along the way, because Pisceans have a short-lived memory. Your realism and control will allow you and your lover to build an actual life together, one that he had trouble building underwater with the Pisces. Stability and partnership are key here.

Aquarius

You are uncomfortable with the thought that she might know more about your man than you do, and the fact that she just might be better able to predict where the two of you will end up is disconcerting, to say the least. You insist that when your man decided to join in a partnership with you, he made a "new beginning," and is now nothing like the man he was when he was with her. This might not be completely true, as human beings rarely reinvent themselves entirely. However, aside from this bit of discomfort, you and the Pisces should be able to get on fairly well. Both of you are dreamers and philosophers, and when your attention is joined, the two of you are able to accomplish a fair number of miracles. You discuss things more with your man than the Pisces ever did, and you are willing to confront difficulties head-on—an attitude that will probably be necessary in sustaining a healthy long-term relationship with your new man.

Pisces

Both of you have so much in common that it would require a lot of energy on both parts to maintain a steady dislike. You understand where she's coming from, even if you don't always like her or agree with her. There is also a strong chance of competition between the two of you, and this alone could foster negativity. Both of you have a jealous streak, and you won't appreciate the Pisces' demand that she retain a place in your man's life. Remember, there are traits of hers that he will miss, and those that he won't. Learn from this, and focus on the positive traits he enjoys while de-emphasizing the bad ones. A wily Fish, you should have no problem being a unique individual in your man's eyes.

About the Author

Rowan Davis was born and raised on the West Coast. Hurricane Katrina, a giant leap of boredom, and a sudden rash decision took her east, where she met her husband and stepdaughter. (A Libran with a Scorpio descendant did what?) She now lives in the state of Texas, surrounded by horses and cowboy hats.

Davis has studied metaphysical subjects for many years, concentrating on astrology and its connections to psychology. She understands that one of the chief concerns of human life is to study and know oneself, and believes that there are many ways for a person to do this. To know yourself and help others to know and love themselves is the highest achievement a person can attain.